MIRACLES R US

THE SACRAMENT OF CONFIRMATION

THE SACRAMENT OF THE ANOINTING OF THE SICK

grace are available through the sacraments. In the Eucharist Christ is fully present as the ordinary bread and wine become his Body and Blood; in confession Christ is there through the priest; in the Sacrament of the Sick, Christ's healing is available. So this book is going to talk about miracles – physical miracles, yes – but the greatest of miracles, the miracle upon the soul, a conversion of heart. Now I know that God does not always heal physically and I cannot say why some people receive physical healing whilst others do not. What I do know is that God always wants to perform miracles in the soul, which is the greater miracle to him, since our souls last for a million, trillion, billion years, for ever and ever, and our earthly bodies are temporary: they will be replaced by an immortal body on the Last Day (see 1 Corinthians 15:35-55). In the Gospels Jesus heals physically to show what He can do in our souls if we give him permission, and what we do now for our souls will have an effect for the good or the bad eternally.

An evident sign that the sacraments are working powerfully in our lives is the fruit they produce, as Jesus taught: 'You will know them by their fruit' (Matthew 7:16). It is great when we experience feelings and emotions through prayer, but it is not the be all and end all if we do not because, unlike our feelings and emotions, our souls are spiritual. The real sign that God is at work in us is the way our lives are transformed – for example, we want to pray more, receive the sacraments more, read the Scriptures more, be more compassionate, caring, stand up for social justice issues, and so on. Jesus said it is not feelings that save us, it is faith (see Luke 7:50).

Bishop Robert Barron reflects on how every sacrament is important for our lives: baptism puts God's divine life in us; confession restores that supernatural life when it is lost; the Eucharist feeds it, confirmation strengthens it, the Sacrament of Marriage and the Sacrament of Holy Orders give it vocational direction, and the Sacrament of the Anointing of the Sick heals it.

In this book, the chapters will not be going in the natural order of how a believer receives the sacraments during their life. The purpose of this book is to show the power and the miraculous that awaits you in each sacrament witnessed by our contributors at different stages/times of their life, but which inevitably began in their own baptism. And no doubt you will see in many cases how the different sacraments intersperse, infuse and complement the great work God has begun in someone through baptism.

So it is a great honour to compile all these great testimonies from very inspiring people who have profoundly experienced God's mercy through the sacraments. And if it has happened for them, it can happen for you!

THE SACRAMENT OF RECONCILIATION
(CONFESSION)

There is no saint without a past, no sinner without a future.

St Augustine

You can fly to heaven on the wings of confession and communion.

St John Bosco

Confession is an act of honesty and courage – an act of entrusting ourselves, beyond sin, to the mercy of a loving and forgiving God.

St Pope John Paul II

Confession Changed My Life

John Pridmore

My name is John Pridmore, I was born in the East End of London, England. At the age of 10, my parents told me to choose who I wanted to live with as they were getting divorced. I think this led me to make a decision inside myself not to love again as the people you love just crush you.

By the age of 27 I had everything that the world says you need to be happy: a penthouse flat, sports cars, and more money than I could spend. The way I got my money was though organised crime. I was involved in major drug deals, protection rackets and violence of all kinds. I used to have a long leather jacket with a sewn-in pocket where I carried a machete. I tell you this not to glory in the past but to reveal the Glory of God.

One night I came home and was aware of a voice speaking to me inside my heart. I knew this voice was God's. At that moment, I said my first prayer and my life began to change. Unbeknown to me, my mother had prayed a novena to St Jude and it was the last day of the novena.

This led me to go on a retreat. My idea of a retreat was to be on a beach with a nice girl, a spliff and a whiskey. As you can imagine, it was not like I thought! The first talk was called 'Give me your wounded heart', and the priest said that each sin we commit is like a wound in our heart. As he was speaking

I was looking at a crucifix and at that moment I knew why Jesus had died for me: He wanted me to be forgiven.

When I came out of the talk, I said a prayer to Our Blessed Mother Mary and asked her what Jesus wanted me to do. I felt her say, 'Go to confession.' I was afraid of what the priest might think, but Mary gave me the courage and I went to confession for over one hour. I was completely honest and did not leave anything out. Then the priest placed his hand on my head and gave me absolution, but it was not his hand, it was Christ's hand, and I knew in my heart that I was forgiven.

I did not know that our hearts are like a glass window: on one side is God's unconditional love pouring down every minute of every day, on the other side are all our sins, so we cannot see how much God loves us. We just see how unworthy of him we are, or even how worthless we are. I took all that sin and tipped it out at the foot of the cross and I was alive again: I could feel the wind on my face, I could hear the birds singing! Those sins had killed me inside, but confession had brought me back to life. When I looked at the priest's eyes, he was crying. He was not judging me, he was Jesus to me.

Now I live and work full-time for Jesus in St Patrick's Community based in Ireland. Many times I am asked by people, 'How do I personally meet Jesus?' I always answer, 'By going to confession and being completely honest.' He always comes to us in the humility of this wonderful sacrament of healing.

I now run a lot of parish missions around the world and at a mission in Derry, Northern Ireland, a man came up to me in his eighties, very emotional, thanking me. He said he had been going to Mass every Sunday since he was 7, but tonight he had met Jesus personally after going to confession for the first time in 48 years. At another mission in Tuam Cathedral a 15-year-old girl said, 'When you came to my school this morning I did not believe in God, but because of what you said, I came tonight, and because of what you said tonight, I went to confession. Not only do I know Jesus is real, but I know He loves me: confession has changed my life.'

Confession changed my life and I thank Jesus every day for the wonder of his mercy. I now go regularly and each time I feel like I am made new again in his love.

John Pridmore (UK) is an ex-London gangster, turned Catholic, who is now an international speaker and author with books including *From Gangland to Promised Land* and *Journey to Freedom*. As a speaker he leads retreats, missions and conferences around the world, including speaking at World Youth Day in Sydney, 2008, before the Vigil service with Pope Benedict XVI. John's story has featured in a number of secular television channels and papers in the UK and Ireland.

Made for More

Leah Darrow

I was born and raised Catholic, but around 15 years old, I began to drift from the practice of my faith. I lost my virginity at 15 years old and unfortunately believed that because of my sins, I no longer had a place in the Catholic Church. I was scared Jesus wouldn't really forgive me and so I slowly did not practise my faith any more. I stopped receiving the sacraments and stopped believing that God would really make me happy. That's when I began to look to the world, to popular culture, to give me what I wanted.

I believed that to be somebody in this world I needed to be rich, famous and beautiful. This attitude led me to audition for the TV show, *America's Next Top Model*. I was chosen to be on cycle 3 and this began my modelling career. After my time on the TV show, *America's Next Top Model*, I decided to move to New York City and pursue modelling full time. I was able to get jobs on the runways in New York City, with major clothing labels and my picture was on the side of taxi cabs and on the billboards in NY Times Square. I thought all of this would make me happy. I thought making a lot of money, fame, and being told I was beautiful would make me feel successful and wanted. But none of these things made me feel happy, at peace or fulfilled. I was surprised that all of the fame, money and popularity ended up making me feel more alone and empty.

I always knew I was made for something great, and thought that my life as a professional model was that 'something great'. I received a phone call from an international magazine one day and they offered me a modelling job that would show people a different side to me. The magazine mentioned that I had always portrayed a nice, safe look but they thought I had something more to offer – that I could be sexy. I agreed to the photoshoot, and thought it would help my career since the magazine is distributed all over the world.

On the day of the photoshoot, I was feeling irritated with my current life. My live-in boyfriend of two years said he loved me but didn't think we were ready for marriage, my party-lifestyle filled with drunken nights was getting old, and I began to question my purpose in life. I was tired of it all but still decided to show up for the magazine photoshoot.

As I got into hair and makeup, they wheeled in a rack of clothes for me to choose from. I did not feel comfortable with any of the outfits and it then became very clear to me that the 'more' they thought I had to offer was being a body to be objectified. I asked for a different set of clothing options to model but was informed that if I did not wear what they offered, I had to leave. I was scared and embarrassed, so I told them it was no problem, picked out a few outfits and the photo shoot began.

Halfway through the shoot, I accidently looked right into the flash from the camera. I asked for a few seconds to regain my focus. During the next few seconds, something happened that I did not expect or plan. As I blinked to regain my focus, I saw an image of myself inside my head – as if a little movie was playing. I was wearing the outfit that I was modelling; however, I had both hands cupped together at my waist which I then raised all the way up as if I was offering them to someone. At this time, I felt a massive feeling of disappointment, and so, brought my hands back down to see what was disappointing. As I looked into my hands, I saw nothing. Nothing. I had nothing to offer, nothing to give. A message was placed on my heart at this time that said to me, 'I made you for more.' I knew that this message was true. I *was* made for more than the life I was currently leading. God had given me so many gifts and talents, but I wasted them all on myself.

The photographer began snapping his fingers saying, 'Leah, focus, let's get back to the shoot.' But I couldn't. Regardless of my past, I knew God was speaking to my heart and reminding me of my dignity and call to greatness. I told the photographer I had to leave and began walking toward the door. Before I walked out of the photo shoot, he said, 'If you leave, you'll be a nobody.' All I could say to him was, 'Do you promise?'

I had been away from the Catholic faith for over ten years and my sins and lifestyle were not bringing me peace. However, the reminder that I had been made for more and the promise of Revelations 21:5, 'Behold, I make all things new', was enough for me to give God another chance.

I knew I needed to change my life but felt overwhelmed with all of the choices of what to do first and how to do it. So, I began first with God. The one step I was sure of was Reconciliation. I needed to reconcile myself with God, to ask for forgiveness and the grace to live a better life. I had not been to the Sacrament of Reconciliation in years and was nervous. But I remembered again, that I was made for more, and so I chose to go to confession immediately.

In that confession, I did not pretend to be a better person than I was; I was honest and gave Christ all of me. In return, Jesus gave me absolute and complete forgiveness, peace, joy and a new beginning. I believe Jesus was speaking to my heart during that photoshoot and He is right – We are made for more.

It is never a question of IF God will forgive you, it is only a question of WHEN – and we control the when. The mercy of Christ awaits all who seek it. I wish I had not been so selfish and prideful in my past so that I could have begun my journey with Christ sooner. But fear kept me from Christ. I beg all Christians: Do not allow fear to steal your joy and your place with Christ. 'We are not the sum of our weaknesses and failures, we are the sum of the Father's love for us and our real capacity to become the image of His Son Jesus' (St Pope John Paul II).

You have been made for more. I pray that you may experience the peace and joy of Christ's mercy and love. And remember, 'The world promises you comfort, but you were not made for comfort. You were made for greatness' (Pope Benedict XVI).

Leah Darrow (USA) is an international speaker, author and former contestant on *America's Next Top Model*. Travelling all round the world with her message that truth, beauty and love are real and need reclaimed. Leah[1] has written her story in the book 'From Top Model to Role Model' and also proclaims this message through articles, podcasts and offering fashion tips available at https://leahdarrow.com.

---

1. The testimony contributed by Leah was originally written as a reflection for the Year of Mercy's '24 hours for the Lord' at the request of the Pontifical Council for the Promotion of the New Evangelization and is used by their kind permission.

Fear Not

Sr Catherine Holum CFR

Fear not, for I have redeemed you; I have called you by
name, you are Mine. (Isaiah 43:1)

As baptised members of the Church, we have a tremendous
dignity. We are children of the Most High God and heirs of the
Kingdom. This is not because we have passed a test or achieved
a prize. It is a pure gift born from the Passion of our Lord
Jesus Christ. Through this gift we have been given freedom
to choose. Some choices lead us to continue to walk in the
light of life, and some choices leave us standing in shadows.

My childhood was full of activity. There was never a dull
moment. My mother, Dianne Holum, is a four-time Olympic
medallist in speed skating and was the coach of three US
Olympic teams. I grew up at the ice rink seeking to imitate
the athletes my mother was coaching. Off the ice, my mother
faithfully took me to Sunday Mass and taught me to pray the
rosary.

When I was 16, my mother had the idea to send my cousin
Jennifer and me on a pilgrimage to the shrine of Our Lady
of Fatima in Portugal. On the first day of our trip, my cousin
and I linked arms as we entered the shrine. Out of the blue,
I heard in my heart, 'You are going to be a Sister!' It was

followed by a profound rush of peace and joy. We soon entered a chapel with Perpetual Adoration of the Blessed Sacrament. As I knelt down to genuflect in the aisle I looked at the Host in the monstrance. Tears of joy began to stream from my eyes as I recognised the 'True Presence' of Jesus. I knew He was real. I knew He was there. It was a life-changing moment.

When I returned from this pilgrimage I started to pray the rosary on the bus on the way to school. I was more reverent at Mass because I knew I was truly receiving Jesus himself in Holy Communion. I also asked the Blessed Mother to pray for my speed skating career. That season I qualified to compete on the most elite American team, travelling on the World Cup circuit. Every time I stepped on the ice I was finishing top eight in the world. The next year I competed in the 1998 Winter Olympic Games in Nagano, Japan, finishing sixth in the 3000 meters and seventh in the 5000 metres. It was a thrilling time as a 17-year-old high school student.

Yet, there was a growing restlessness in my heart because I knew there was more to life for me than sports. With great peace and no regrets, I retired after the Olympics. I went on to study Photography at the School of the Art Institute of Chicago. However, it was a difficult transition from speed skating to art school. The hardest part was trying to stay close to Jesus. I continued to go to Sunday Mass to make myself feel good. When I felt really guilty about something I sometimes went to confession. I knew what was right and wrong but there was no real desire to change. I never stopped believing in God, but in many ways I was not putting him first. By the end of my degree, I had completely forgotten about the call I received to be a Sister.

After I graduated, I moved out to Denver to live with my mother. She invited me to come with her one Saturday to pray the rosary outside an abortion clinic. Through the faithful Catholics I met praying peacefully that day, I heard about 'Crossroads'. They are a group of young people who dedicate their summer to walk across America for the pro-life movement. As the Crossroads walkers passed through Denver the next week, I found myself sitting in a church hall listening to the testimonies of these young, zealous Catholics. I was deeply impressed by their radiant joy. I had never seen anything like it before and wanted to experience it myself. That night before I went to sleep a prayer rose up in my heart as I lay in bed. 'Lord, what do you want for me?' I had never invited the Lord into my life in this way. Within two days I joined Crossroads, put on a Pro-Life T-shirt and started walking across America with twelve young people and an Australian priest. Through daily Mass, offering up prayers and sacrifices, and through the witness of these new friends, my heart was gently being purified to hear the Lord's voice once again. I began to realise there were a lot of things that needed to change in my life, and this time I actually wanted to change. True contrition began to stir in my heart. I knew I needed to go to confession. One weekend we were attending a young adult retreat and they had confession available in the evening. My heart was thumping as I stood nervously in line. I had a lot to say and I wasn't sure how it would all come out. The priest was so kind and understanding. After my confession, I felt a weight fall off my shoulders and there was lightness in my step. It was a new beginning. The Lord had truly heard my prayer and I discovered what He wanted for me – a pure heart. It is only with this purity of heart that I would be able to hear him calling me to my true vocation as a Religious Sister.

Not only did I recall the Lord's words to me in Fatima when I was 16 years old after that confession, but I saw the sacrament in a whole different way. It developed into an important part of my life and I started to go regularly. Confession is an opportunity to begin again and to receive the strength we need to be faithful to Christ. With every confession, I have experienced Jesus pull me out of the shadow of sin and into his marvellous light. St Pope John Paul II once wrote that 'conversion is the most concrete expression of the working of love and the presence of mercy in the human world' (*Dives in Misericordia,* 6). Jesus, who is Love and Mercy Itself, is waiting for us in the Sacrament of Confession. Let us not be afraid to meet him there.

Sr Catherine Holum CFR (USA) joined the Community of the Franciscan Sisters of the Renewal in 2003 in the Bronx, New York. She currently resides at St Clare Convent in Leeds, England. The Franciscan Sisters of the Renewal, founded in 1988, live a common life of prayer, serve the very poor in their neighbourhoods, and are engaged in an extensive evangelisation apostolate.

Confession
Editor

A number of years back before I was a priest, I was in my home parish church saying some prayers when a lady walked in whom I had never seen before. She was middle-aged with black hair, very pretty and well-dressed, but there seemed to be something bothering her. I couldn't help noticing her body language and her manner, so I approached her and asked, 'Is everything okay?' She responded, 'No.' Then she told me that for the past twenty years she had been an alcoholic and because of it she had wrecked two marriages, liquidated two businesses, and she was not even faithful to the person she was with at the moment. But most tragically of all, her two grown-up children now wanted nothing to do with her. She looked at me with desperation asking what she should do. I was not sure how to respond so I just shared with her about a time in my own life when I was struggling with depression but confession changed everything for me. I told her how I had experienced God's healing power, love and mercy in that sacrament and that it might have a similar effect on her.

She asked me when confession was available. I explained the time slots for Saturdays and she said she would think about coming back then. In an instant I knew this was a moment for the taking, that if she left today I may never see her again. I blurted out, 'But you could go to confession now if you want.' She said, 'What do you mean?'

I replied, 'I could run and get the priest next door and see if he would be willing to hear your confession.' She said, 'Let me think about it.' I replied that while she thought about it I would see if the priest was in. Running to the presbytery, I knocked on the door, and when the priest opened it I said, 'Father, there's a lady in there who is an alcoholic and has not gone to confession in over twenty years. Would you be willing to hear her confession?'

He agreed and prepared to go into the confessional. I went back to the church and explained to the lady that the priest was happy to hear her confession and that when the light went on outside of the confessional door that meant the priest was ready. He was ready to invite the mercy, forgiveness and power of God into her life, that this could really help her and be a true changing point. It was up to her. She was still unsure so I left her to it. The light outside the confessional went on and she got up and went in. I stayed outside praying. When she came out, although it was the same person, there was something different about her. It was like shackles had come off, she had been released from her chains and she was free and her body language and manner

> If you forgive the sins of any, they are forgiven them; if you retain the sins of any, they are retained.
>
> *John 20:23*

showed it as she smiled. I suggested we say a short prayer together and then she left.

Fast-forward to about 18 months later. I was driving down the road in an area near the church and saw this same lady walking down the road... may I emphasise walking, not staggering! I pulled over and said, 'Remember me?' She did, so I offered her a lift, and as we were driving along I enquired how she had been. She said, 'Since that day in the church I have been to a clinic and dried out, but more importantly I am back in touch with my two grown-up children.' She went on to say, 'Things aren't perfect, but they're getting there.'

> God alone can forgive sins. Jesus could say 'Your sins are forgiven' (Mark 2:5) only because he is the Son of God. And priests can forgive sins in Jesus' place only because Jesus has given them that authority.
>
> *YouCat, 228 [1441-1442]*

I share that story for two reasons: first of all, to reveal the power of the Sacrament of Reconciliation; and secondly, to highlight the words of Jesus himself – the truth sets you free (John 8:32). God wants to heal our wounds and brokenness. But we need to step out of the darkness into the light. It is like going to the doctor's: a doctor cannot treat a disease you deny you have. But give the doctor specifics – a sore head, stomach ache, cannot lift my right arm – he or she treats and prescribes accurately. It is exactly the same with God, He cannot treat any sins, mistakes, brokenness we have if we deny them and refuse to surrender them to him. There was a time in my life when I was really struggling with depression through OCD (Obsessive Compulsive Disorder) – in case you're not sure what that is, I'll give one example: I couldn't leave a place without making sure all the windows were shut, all the doors were locked and all the drawers were in. That may not sound like a big deal to you, but try checking out of a hotel! But a priest walked into my life at that time, it was an answer to a prayer, a priest I could trust with the darkness that was going in within me. I confided in him and he invited me to go to confession. I did not want to go, but I thought I had nothing to lose and everything to gain, so I did. I thought if I'm doing it, I'm doing it right, I need to get rid of everything that's on my heart. And at the end of this confession the priest put his hand over my head and said the words of absolution/forgiveness and as he was saying those words I felt this incredible breeze of heat literally rip through every core of my being interiorly – I had not known peace like it. And I knew God was there, helping me, pouring out his love and mercy.

Is God angry with me?

God is not some wrathful, vengeful God watching every move you make so He can notice every time you trip up. The reason God does not want us to sin is because when we do, we hurt those people closest to him – ourselves! Think about it: we are made in the image and likeness of God (Genesis 1:26-27), which means were made to shimmer and shine, as Jesus said, to be a light to the world (Matthew 5:14). But when we sin we dent our own image of ourselves and then we can start to make the mistake of believing the lie that we are unlovable. God isn't angry with us. He loves us. He knows that sin separates us from the grace and love of our Father-God who wants to work so magnificently in us.

God just wants to take away your pain so you can be free

John Pridmore tells the story of getting a thorn stuck in his finger when he was a child. He did not want to show his mum, thinking she would pull it out and it would be very painful. So for three days he hid his finger from her, but eventually his finger was in that much pain he had to show her. Immediately she took out the thorn: his finger felt better and the healing process began. He thought to himself, 'What an idiot, I have been in pain these last three days and all my mum wanted to do is to take away the pain.' That is exactly the same with confession: all God wants to do is to take away our pain, reach into our hearts and remove the thorns that limit us and stop us from being free. Imagine if John had kept that thorn in his finger for months, even years, what would have happened to his finger and hand? Likewise unconfessed sins that we carry around for years can become barriers and blockades to God's love and all he wants to give us, when he just wants us to be free. You deserve that love.

Who should go to confession?

According to St Paul 'all have sinned and fall short of the glory of God' (Romans 3:23). He laments, in one of his letters, that the good he knows he should do, he doesn't do, and the bad he should never do, he does do (Romans 7:15-17). This also fits with the Scripture which says that even the just person sins seven times a day (Proverbs 24:16). But what is a serious sin?

I want to give an example of what the Church classifies as mortal/serious sin. This is when someone intentionally, with full knowledge and full consent, deliberately makes a decision to commit a grave offence (sin) – in other words, turning your back on God. Here's the thing: imagine standing in a river that comes up to your ankles. This river is meant to represent all God's love, mercy and power working in your life, which is not meant to stop at your ankles. It is meant to rise to your waist, to your shoulders, in fact to totally consume you, so that God's divine love, mercy and power is in control, leading and guiding you. But imagine committing a mortal sin – like one of the Big Ten (the Ten Commandments – Exodus 20). The water evaporates and disperses until once again you are left with it just by your ankles: you are now struggling, trying, to live your life with limited grace. But confession restores the river

> Three conditions are necessary for penance: contrition, which is sorrow for sin, together with a purpose of amendment; confession of sins without any omission; and satisfaction by means of good works.
>
> *St Thomas Aquinas*

and fills you with God's love, mercy and goodness. To put it another way (to take inspiration from Scott Hahn) it's like throwing the most amazing party in your heart with a joy and peace that cannot be matched. Serious sin, on the other hand, is like turning off the music, announcing there's no more dancing and ordering the Trinity out of your heart.

Your weaknesses do not define you and they certainly should not master you. If you haven't already, take hold of the chance to go to confession: it will change your life. And when you confess, get rid of everything! Confession is a real opportunity to be transformed. St Catherine of Siena believed going to confession is receiving 'baptism in the Spirit'. Even if you are not sure that God exists go to confession and experience the mercy of a God who loved you so much He did not want to give you up without a fight.

Where can I receive God's mercy?

I have heard confessions in the most unusual places. Once at the Edinburgh Festival, when people spotted me with my priestly collar and assumed it was a costume, they kept asking, 'Which show are you in, where's your venue?' I replied: 'Your local Catholic Church, once a day, twice on a Sunday, four-star reviews, I can get you front-row seats!' But one performer from the Festival who noticed my collar asked for confession.

On another occasion in Ireland I got a taxi to morning Mass. On the way to the church the taxi driver and I chatted socially about a number of issues, but faith was not mentioned. When we arrived at the church, with one foot on the tarmac and the other still in the car, I said to the taxi driver, 'I'll pray for you during Mass this morning.' He responded by saying, 'How does a person know if he's forgiven?'

I got back in the taxi and we had a conversation about God's inexpressible, unconditional love. After our chat, he asked me, 'Father, would you hear my confession?' And I said to this taxi driver, 'Certainly, but can you just turn off your meter otherwise it's going to cost me a fortune.' But seriously, God dished out his mercy to that man, who I'm sure when he woke up that morning never expected God to impact his life in the way that he did that day.

> Confession heals, confession justifies, confession grants pardon of sin, all hope consists in confession; in confession there is a chance for mercy.
>
> *St Isidore of Seville*

Jesus showed his mercy to everyone and although He spent a significant amount of time in synagogues, He also was out and about: on top of hills, by lakesides, in the market squares, at dinner parties. His mercy was not limited to specific times and places but was for everyone, even going to find those who needed it most.

Mercy on a Bus

I was fortunate to help in my diocese (the Diocese of Salford) with a project for the Year of Mercy: a Mercy Bus. Under the patronage of Bishop John Arnold the concept was a double-decker bus specially designed with images of Pope Francis, priests hearing confession or giving a blessing, and so on, to advertise God's love and mercy. The Mercy Bus parked up in town and city centres and shopping malls with priests on-board available for confession, blessings or just a chat. They were accompanied by young-adult volunteers who played live music and invited people on board. And if you came on board and paid a bus fare, after your confession we dropped you off home. We didn't, I'm just kidding. One of the most inspiring things that resulted from this project was people returning to the Sacrament of Reconciliation after 10, 20, 30 years and having a profound encounter with God's mercy. Some said they were going to return to Mass. One man contacted our office and had a conversation with one of our group leaders, Lorraine. He said he had not been to confession in 20 years, that he didn't feel he could go to the Sacrament of Reconciliation in a church but that he was going to go that weekend on the Bus. Lorraine asked him what prompted his decision. He said, 'Because you are not waiting for me to come to you, you are coming out and meeting me where I am.' The visible outreach of the Bus was enough to encourage people to seek what they had previously been so afraid and reluctant to seek: God's unconditional mercy and love. I once heard a phrase, 'Sometimes you don't wait for your ship to sail in, you swim out to it.' Well, similarly, let's not wait for our Bus to pull up. Take the initiative and go to confession.

Why go to a priest in confession?

Because it is Jesus Christ who sends us priests, He is the one who gives the power and authority for them to be 'other Christs'. By merit of their ordination, when the bishop lays his hand on the heads of the priests, their souls ontologically change, for ever to conform to Christ's soul. So whenever a priest carries out ministry, he does so in the person of Christ himself. Therefore, in confession, it is Christ who reaches out and forgives and heals through the priest. What is said and confessed in this sacrament is between you and Christ: this is known as the seal of confession (see CCC 1467). A Catholic priest does not and cannot repeat any of what is said and confessed. If the priest repeated what was said and confessed he would have his faculties/powers as a priest taken from him.

> Penance is the second baptism, the baptism of tears.
>
> *St Gregory Nazianzen*

Sometimes I speak to people who believe they have done something so bad that they are too ashamed to confess it. But God's mercy is greater than the worst thing you have ever done and we priests do not judge you when you come to confess. In fact, the more honest and upfront you are, the more a priest loves you and wants to reconcile you with God and the Church. I once asked a very holy man if there is one sin that cannot be forgiven. He said, 'Yes. Believing that nothing can be forgiven.' Think about it, God cannot give you anything you refuse to accept.

Let us take some case studies of God's mercy. Imagine if someone was a fraudster, a two-faced liar who manipulated people to get their way, cheating them of their money and possessions – could they be forgiven? Or what about a thief, someone who steals, hurts, judges and accuses others but not their own guilty deeds – could they be forgiven? Or what about an adulterer? Someone who has acted on selfish lust and pride with the marital act outside of marriage, causing deep pain and hurt – could they be forgiven? Well yes! Jesus forgave them all: they are Zacchaeus the tax collector (Luke 19:1-10), the Good Thief (Luke 23:32-43) and the woman caught in adultery (John 8:1-11).

> God esteems repentance so highly that the slightest repentance in the world, as long as it is genuine, causes him to forget any kind of sin, so that even the devils would have all their sins forgiven, if only they could have remorse.
>
> *St Francis de Sales*

They each experienced the mercy and loving presence of God, knew it was real and let him transform their lives: all by meeting a God who was ready to forgive.

There is only one condition: you have to want the mercy. God is a gentleman, He does not go where He is not invited. Everybody who encountered Christ in the Gospels all started out from a place of needing his mercy, and then they encountered him. The saints show us that God just doesn't want us to meet him once, but to continue encountering him and discovering more of his love and mercy for our lives. So, may I boldly suggest you receive this sacrament regularly?

We were born for greatness. When you go to confession and have been as honest as you could, when the priest puts his hand over your head - it's not his hand but Christ's hand – and you hear the words of absolution and forgiveness which the priest says over you at the end – in that moment your soul becomes as pure, as white, as beautiful and as ready for heaven as it was on the day of your baptism! God has raised his game, are you ready to raise yours?

How Good It Feels to Come Back to Him

Charles Whitehead

In common with nearly all young Catholics, my first experience of the Sacrament of Reconciliation, or confession as we knew it, was in connection with making my First Holy Communion at the age of 7. I was prepared for both these sacraments by the sisters from a local convent who helped our parish priest with the weekly 'Sunday School' – normally held on a Saturday afternoon.

My memories of their teaching on confession are very simple; whenever I did anything wrong or was naughty in any way, I had to remember it so that I could tell Father about it when I went to confession, ask for and receive God's forgiveness, and then seriously do whatever penance I was given. I then had to take great care to avoid this particular 'occasion of sin' in the future. Confession at that time in the late 1940s took place, of course, in a 'box', and I always hoped that Father would not recognise who it was giving his short list of very predictable sins which varied little from one confession to the next.

At the age of 10 I went as a boarder to Stonyhurst, the Jesuit school in Lancashire, where confession was timetabled into our weekly class programme. It took place on Saturday mornings during normal class time and this gave it some attraction, as we escaped from the classroom for a few minutes. The whole class went one after another – we didn't have any choice. When I moved on from the preparatory school to the main college at the age of 13, confession was still timetabled and we were strongly encouraged to go every week, but with less rigidity and pressure than when I was younger.

As I look back on this experience, I have to say that it did not leave me with a love for the Sacrament of Reconciliation. Rather I saw it as a slightly uncomfortable necessity to be undertaken as infrequently as possible. I certainly understood what it was all about but I was not fully convinced that the only way to receive God's forgiveness was through this rather embarrassing ritual. Surely, I could just express my regret and sorrow to my Heavenly Father in private prayer? After all, that's what the Protestants mostly did, and I was sure they were forgiven. So with such feelings in my heart, it will come as no surprise to you to hear that when I left school and went on to Durham University, the practice of this particular sacrament effectively stopped. The Jesuits had done a great job in ensuring I had an extensive intellectual understanding of my Catholic faith, and I was well able to explain and defend it in student discussions, usually in pubs over a few pints. The problem was that my faith was totally intellectual, so my heart, and therefore my life, remained largely unaffected. In this situation, the regular practice of my faith through the sacraments declined to an occasional appearance at Sunday Mass. I never lost my faith, but its regular practice was another matter.

This was all to change in 1976 when I was 34 years old, married to Sue, an atheist, for ten years, and with our first two children. We had married in a Catholic church and both children had been baptised and were attending the local Catholic school, when we were invited by some friends to join an ecumenical home group of Anglicans, Baptists and Catholics to talk about our Christian faith. Largely through the example and remarkable witness of a Baptist couple, Sue came to faith quite dramatically, gave up her atheism, and returned to her Anglican roots. Shortly after this, my very academic faith was set on fire when I experienced the presence and power of the Holy Spirit in my life and everything changed. What happened to me was that I experienced baptism in the Holy Spirit, and the graces I received at my baptism became fully active in me as the Lord poured his Spirit upon me in new ways. One of the first results was that I decided to 'get right with God' and to receive the Sacrament of Reconciliation again after a gap of many years. A particular verse of Scripture really came home to me:

If we say we have no sin, we deceive ourselves, and the truth is not in us. (1 John 1:8)

Finding myself near Westminster Cathedral one lunch time, I went in to pray and discovered a number of people sitting waiting for confession. So I joined the line. The priest in the box had a rather loud voice but I did my best to ignore it as I thought about all the sins I needed to confess. When my turn came and I entered the confessional box, I became aware through the thin veil, of an elderly, serious-looking priest who, to my surprise, was wearing a biretta on his head and had the highest white dog collar I had ever seen. I began to confess in the words I had learned as a child: 'Bless me, Father, for I have sinned. It is fourteen years since my last confession.'

If I was expecting an encouraging response, a warm 'Welcome home!' I was sadly mistaken. 'Good heavens! Fourteen years! What stopped you coming then?' was what I heard. Undeterred, I began to confess my sins, only to be interrupted by a succession of gasps of surprise and frequent remarks like 'Good heavens!', 'Well I never!', 'Whatever next!' and more. My experience was totally different to that of the Prodigal Son described in Luke chapter 15. There was certainly nothing that resembled music, feasting or song! But I persevered and made it to the end, only to receive a lecture on my failings and a very impressive penance. As I returned to a pew I noticed that the number of penitents awaiting their turn seemed to have decreased considerably, and from the sympathetic looks I received from those remaining, I gathered they had heard the comments and shared in my discomfort.

Now obviously my experience was exceptional and bears no resemblance to the normal reception given to a repentant sinner, no matter how long they have been away from the sacrament. But in it all, the wonderful thing was that I experienced the transforming power of the sacrament. I felt changed, cleansed, transformed and released to live a new life of faith. The miraculous power of the Sacrament of Reconciliation broke through all the human failings of both confessor and penitent, releasing an unforgettable torrent of grace into my heart and life. None of my past experiences had prepared me for this! I left the cathedral after completing my lengthy penance a totally new person and I have never looked back. As Pope Francis expresses it:

> How good it feels to come back to him whenever we are lost! Let me say this once more: God never tires of forgiving us; we are the ones who tire of seeking his mercy. (*Evangelii Gaudium*, 3)

My next experience of confession was equally transformational and could hardly have been more different. I was attending a conference and one evening asked a priest if he would hear my confession. We sat side by side in a quiet corner, he asked about my faith, my spiritual journey, and we talked through everything that was both good and a weakness in my life. He ended what had been an hour talking together by laying hands on me and praying over me for ten minutes. On both occasions, which could hardly have been more different, I knew the miraculous transforming power of the Sacrament of Reconciliation.

As *YouCat*, 226 reminds us:

It does not seem like a modern thing to go to confession; it can be difficult and may cost a great deal of effort at first. But it is one of the greatest graces that we can receive again and again in our life – it truly renews the soul, completely unburdens it, leaving it without the debts of the past, accepted in love, and equipped with new strength. God is merciful, and he desires nothing more earnestly than for us, too, to lay claim to his mercy. Someone who has gone to confession turns a clean, new page in the book of his life.

The approach of every priest will be quite different; my attitude and the state of my spiritual life may vary considerably from one occasion to the next; but the power of God, flowing into me through the grace of the sacrament, is unchanging.

It's always the same – supernatural, miraculous and life-transforming every time.

What a gift to us!

Charles Whitehead (UK) has taught and evangelised Christian spirituality and teaching all over the world and authored several books. He has served as Chairman of the International Catholic Charismatic Office in Rome, where he met with St Pope John Paul II on many occasions. He and his wife Sue are the founders of 'Celebrate' Catholic Charismatic family conferences throughout the UK.

A Divine Gift

Fr Joseph Evans

In George Bernanos' novel *La Joie* ('Joy'), the great French author has one of his characters say the following: 'We all have our secrets, a whole load of secrets which end up rotting in the conscience, being consumed there, slowly, slowly.'

One of the purposes for which God gave us the Sacrament of Confession is precisely so that this grim situation does not happen to us. That is the first thing we must say about this sacrament: it is a divine gift, not an imposition or a means by which the Church seeks to control us. It is truly a liberation. A person who goes regularly to confession gradually grows in freedom. The rot does not accumulate and what remains is transformed into growth-giving fertilizer.

We are progressively freed from the defects which chain us down and the corruption which otherwise would infect our soul. Imagine a yoghurt left months at the back of a dark cupboard and you get an idea of a soul which goes months and months without confession.

It is interesting that although this sacrament is known by a number of different names, the Sacrament of Penance, the Sacrament of Reconciliation, and so on, it is most commonly called confession. This is because people know what is really crucial, though most difficult, in this sacrament: the speaking out, the confession of our sins.

But this speaking out is precisely what Our Lord called 'coming to the light' (John 3:21). By exposing our sins to the judgement of the Church through her priests, they are opened to God's light. And one of the best ways to cure any wound is to expose it to the healing rays of the warm sunlight.

Our Lord, as I once read, could have said: 'Dig a hole in the garden, put your head in the hole and say your sins into the hole, and you will be forgiven.' He didn't, because having become a man himself, He knew us. He knew our need to get things off our chest, to share them with others, to receive advice and encouragement, and above all to hear with certainty that we are forgiven: 'I absolve you from your sins in the name of the Father...' With those words so many chains of anxiety slip off us.

Confession is all about love. God's love for us and our desire to love him. The more you love the more you feel a need to say sorry, the more little things matter. Frequent confession thus becomes a path to healing, to spiritual progress and to growth in divine love. It is not just the Father's hug for the Prodigal Son on his return, but entering ever more into the tender arms of infinite compassion.

Fr Joseph Evans (UK) is a priest of the Catholic prelature Opus Dei and a member of its Regional Council for Great Britain. He has been working with young people and university students for over 20 years. He is also a teacher in Scared Scripture in which he holds a doctorate. As a former journalist, he helped to start *Reach Out!* a mentoring project to help disadvantaged children in Manchester which now operates in Glasgow and London.

A New Person
Meg Hunter-Kilmer

Every good thing in my life is the product of one confession when I was 13 years old. Any joy I feel, any meaning my life has can be traced to that day. Nearly all of my friendships are a direct result of walking – reluctantly – into the confessional and walking out a new person.

It certainly wasn't my intention to go to confession that weekend. If you'd asked me, I expect I would have told you that I didn't think I'd ever go to confession. I'd been once before, you see, and hadn't thought much of it.

What I probably wouldn't have mentioned was that in my one confession, way back when I was 7, I hadn't known what to say. What had I really done that was so wrong? Not wanting to look stupid, I decided my best bet would be to make something up. So, in my first confession, I lied to the priest. I made up one sin, said only that, and got out of there as quickly as I could, glad to know that confession is something you only have to do once in your life.

You won't be surprised to hear that faith wasn't a big part of my life. My family went to Mass on Sundays, but I did my utmost to avoid going or to avoid paying attention if dragged there. I didn't go to Catholic school. I didn't pray. I'd jumped head first into a life without God and I wasn't turning back.

At first, I was mostly just disinterested; later, almost defiant in my sin. And somewhere in there, I began to listen to the voice of the culture that told me you had to be stupid to believe in God, that only people who don't think are Christians. I was a smart kid, so I figured that meant I didn't believe in God. By the time I was 11, I'd decided I was an atheist. With all the consistency of an 11-year-old, there were certainly times that I was much closer to an agnostic and other times that I was something like a Christian, but in general this much was true: I didn't buy this Jesus nonsense and I wasn't interested in giving it a shot.

The world will tell you that atheism is a sweet deal. After all, if there's no God, there's no sin. There's no guilt, there's no shame. The trouble is, there's still guilt and there's still shame, there's just no mercy. There's no healing. Whatever ugly things you've done, you're going to carry them for ever.

There's also no meaning. There's no purpose. Though I couldn't exactly have expressed it at 12, I knew deep down that if I was right and God was a fairy tale, then I was nothing more than a random series of chemical reactions. My life meant nothing and eventually I'd die and disintegrate and that would be the end.

I remember waking up in the morning thinking, 'What's the point? Why bother getting out of bed in the morning?' I was profoundly aware that I was never going to be enough, that I was never going to be happy. No matter what I did, I was always going to mess up, I was always going to hurt people. I took a long, sober look at life and decided that people just aren't happy. Not consistently, anyway. And at 12 years old I resigned myself to my fate: an empty, meaningless life in which I spent my time trying to forget the aching hunger that this world would never satisfy.

And then, that fateful retreat.

I spent the entire retreat rolling my eyes. I wasn't interested in the talks or the activities. I thought the whole thing was a waste of time. Then we went through an examination of conscience and my boredom turned to anger. Who did these people think they were? They couldn't tell me how to live. It was my body, it was my life, it was my choice. This whole ridiculous list of sins was just the Church's attempt to control me.

Then, one by one, every girl in my small group got up to go to confession. As little as I wanted to go, I cared far more what these girls thought of me (entirely unaware that nobody cared if I went to confession or not). So off I went, spurred on by imaginary peer pressure – neither perfect nor imperfect contrition, but apparently God decided it was good enough.

I walked into that confessional thinking I was just going to say a couple of things to some priest and then move on with my life. But as I sat there, listing the sins of the past six years, something in me changed. I don't know if I became aware of God's mercy or just my own sinfulness, but I began to cry. As my confession went on, I cried harder and harder until

I was crying so hard I couldn't breathe. God bless Fr Mark Moretti, he kept interrupting me to make small talk so that I could calm down enough to breathe. I choked and sobbed my way through what I'm sure was a very imperfect confession and then – mercy upon mercy – Jesus Christ himself reached down to take my sins upon himself and make me new again.

In that confession, I experienced mercy that I never knew was possible. It turned out I wasn't talking to 'some priest', I was kneeling at the foot of the cross, giving Jesus Christ the hammer that *I* used to nail him there and He was reaching out his pierced hands to me saying, 'I still love you. I still want you.'

In that moment, the God I had turned my back on went down on his knees before me to beg me to love him. And, miracle of miracles, I did.

Confession shouldn't work like that. Someone who isn't sorry shouldn't be able to read a list of sins and be transformed. It's not magic, after all. But it is miraculous.

I remember walking out of that confession and standing underneath the Virginia sky thinking, 'Well, shoot. If Jesus is God, that changes everything. It doesn't just change my Sunday morning, it changes my Saturday night. It changes the way I talk, the way I dress, it changes everything.' Not because suddenly there was this list of rules to follow but because in that sacrament I had met a God who loved me so deeply that

He was glad to die for me. And if I was that deeply loved, my life had to look different.

If you'd asked me a few months later, I would have told you that my life had been moving the right direction and this was just a push to move faster toward God. But it's not true. My life was going nowhere. My feeling of emptiness wasn't going to be filled and I wasn't going to turn to God. Whether I considered myself a Christian before that weekend or not, I'm quite sure that if I hadn't had that experience in confession, it wouldn't have been long before I left the Church for good.

In that moment, God spoke to my heart and told me how deeply He loved me. My whole life changed. I began to pray. I got involved in every youth group at my Church and every Christian group at my school. When I got my driver's licence, I started going to daily Mass. I studied theology at a Catholic college. I became a religion teacher, then an itinerant missionary. And while I certainly won't pretend that being a Christian is easy, it is *good*. There is peace and joy and glory that the world just can't offer.

Mine is an extreme story, and yet it's the story of every confession. Every single time a sinner walks into the confessional, a miracle happens. St Augustine said, 'The conversion of a sinner into a just man is a greater miracle than the creation of heaven and earth.'

And truly, the only difference between a sinner and a saint is one confession. I'm profoundly blessed that the miracle of confession touched my heart that day; truly, it's made all the difference. But every time a sinner is absolved, it's a miracle. If you're looking to experience the power of God, may I recommend dumping your sins in the confessional? You've got nothing to lose and everything to gain.

Meg Hunter-Kilmer (USA) is a hobo missionary. After two theology degrees from Notre Dame and five years as a high-school religion teacher, she quit her job in 2012 to live out of her car and preach the Gospel to anyone who would listen. Fifty states and twenty countries later, this seems to have been a less ridiculous decision than it initially seemed. She blogs at www.piercedhands.com.

Our Lord Himself I saw in... this venerable
sacrament... I felt as if my chains fell, as those
of St Peter at the touch of the divine messenger.
My God, what new scenes for my soul.

St Elizabeth Ann Seton

Love covers over a multitude of sins.

1 Peter 4:8

It must be recalled that... this reconciliation with
God leads, as it were, to other reconciliations,
which repair the other breaches caused by sin.
The forgiven penitent is reconciled with himself in
his inmost being, where he regains his innermost
truth. He is reconciled with his brethren whom
he has in some way offended and wounded. He is
reconciled with the Church. He is reconciled with
all creation.

St Pope John Paul II

THE BLESSED SACRAMENT (EUCHARIST)

There is nothing so great my children, as the Eucharist! Put all the good works in the world against one good Communion; they will be like a grain of dust beside a mountain.

St Jean Vianney

If when He lived in this world, He healed the sick by the mere touch of His garments, what doubt is there but that He will perform miracles, since He is so intimately within us, if we have a lively faith; and that He will grant us what we ask of Him, while He is in our house?

St Teresa of Avila

And they devoted themselves to the apostles' teaching and fellowship, to the breaking of bread and the prayers.

Acts 2:42

A Real Person

Sr Briege McKenna OSC

I am very aware that in the healing ministry God heals in a variety of ways: divine intervention through the sacraments, where God miraculously touches lives and heals them (a ministry that I'm called to with Fr Kevin Scallon); by giving us doctors, or people to help us find doctors; through medication. God works in all these ways to heal. Here I share with you a few true stories which I would call miracles of the Lord.

The first story was told to me by a mother who came to see me about a month ago:

Sr Briege, she said, this happened quite a while back and I've never had a chance to tell you. You and Fr Kevin were ministering during a parish mission in the United States when my little boy was 9 years of age and had about 20 epileptic seizures a day. I was told that there would be a parish mission with a Eucharistic healing service so I brought little Nick. When Fr Kevin held up the monstrance you told the people, 'This is Jesus,' and reminded them what Jesus clearly told St Faustina: '"I'm not an object, I'm a living Person." This is the same Risen Jesus and I stress this.'

Well my little 9-year-old was really listening. He knew that every day he had to take all kinds of medication, he couldn't play soccer, he couldn't play any sports because of the disease. As he was listening to you he was also looking at Jesus in the monstrance; he was begging Jesus and I could see that it was affecting him in his faith. After the service we went home but he didn't say anything. The next morning when I had to give him his medicine he said, 'I don't want it.' I told him he had to take it as he couldn't go to school without it. He said, 'Mummy, no, because I'm healed. Last night Jesus was in the church and He told me I was healed when He was walking around.'

I looked at him and part of me was so scared and I asked, 'Are you sure?' He answered, 'But Mummy, do you not really believe that's Jesus? Because in the middle of the night He reminded me again.'

Today my son is an engineer and he has never had a seizure from that night at the parish mission. And he is completely changed.

The next miracle happened in a different way. A man who came to a mission we were giving was driving us to the airport afterwards and he told us his story:

A few years ago I was given a month to live, eaten away with cancer, no hope, when my friend said, 'You should come to a mission offered by Sr Briege and Fr Kevin. There's anointing for the sick and a healing service where they talk about the Eucharist.' I knew the mission was far away – two-and-a-half, three-hours travel – but I thought, well I'm dying and I'm going to be miserable anyway, so I might as well go. There were confessions the first night so I went to confession and then you prayed with me, Sr Briege. I had a wonderful encounter with Jesus in the Sacrament of Confession, attended the Eucharistic healing service afterwards and then went home. The next morning I got a phone call from the biggest pharmaceutical research company in America. I don't have a clue how they got my name but they said, 'Your name has been picked out with several other people who have radical cancer and no hope. Would you be willing to give us permission to experiment with a new drug which has just been brought out?' Something inside me said, 'That's why you went last night because I'm going to give you an avenue for healing.' Twenty of us cooperated with this treatment and I survived, completely healed through it, and I knew that it was because the Lord wanted to show that people who spend their lives trying to find cures for people through research are instruments of God. I was healed to give glory to God for the research of science and medicine because it completely eradicated my cancer.

People think of me as having a healing ministry but really it is through the sacraments of the Church that God heals. This is what I speak a lot about. Rarely have I been present when these miracles happen and that's the mercy of God because the Lord takes me away from the church or wherever we are ministering so the glory goes directly to the Lord and the sacraments.

Every sacrament is a door to Jesus. There are seven doors (and here I'm quoting Fr Kevin) and behind every door Jesus is waiting to minister to you. In baptism, the door opens for you to receive Jesus into your whole life so He can occupy your life, your soul, everything. In the Sacrament of Penance, you walk into the Jesus of Mercy; in Holy Communion you walk into Jesus the Bread of Life; in marriage you walk into Jesus who will unite your two hearts with his in the sacrament that makes him present. Holy Orders makes the priest so united to Jesus that he acts 'in the person of Christ'. People are looking all over for extraordinary things and this is why I tell Catholics, 'If you really believed, you would know that every single day the same Person who healed the blind man is in the church. If a doctor said, "Go and take chemotherapy because it's going to save your life," people would flock to the doctors. They believe the doctor, but they don't believe Jesus who said, "Come to me."'

The same with confession. The first extraordinary miracle that I saw from that sacrament was an unseen one, in the soul. In the western United States a man came to a mission looking for me to pray with his child but there was no 'praying with people' that night, it was the Sacrament of Reconciliation. He heard us speaking about confession and meeting Jesus and he went to confession. But because his reason for coming to the mission was to get me to pray he left disappointed. This man, a bank manager, had a withered leg from polio. Two days after his confession his wife called Fr Kevin to tell him about her husband's leg: the muscle that had died through polio had started developing and by the end of the mission he had a perfect leg. By that time the whole bank had come to the mission!

Today I went to visit a priest who is dying. I told him never be afraid to ask the Lord for a miracle because you may not get physical healing, but you'll get even better: when you pray for miracles there's an opening to God who pours in his grace and that grace can either flood your body and physically heal you or it can flood your soul and prepare you for the Kingdom. It happens whether it's for this life or for the next.

Sr Briege McKenna OSC (Ireland) entered the Sisters of St Clare at the age of 15. Known throughout the world for her healing and preaching ministry and ministry to priests along with Fr Kevin Scallon CM (Intercession for Priests). Sr Briege who has travelled extensively around the World giving retreats and conferences is also the author of *Miracles Do Happen*. She is the 2009 recipient of the Award for Outstanding Catholic Leadership from the Catholic Leadership Institute.

'He Lives in Us'

Jean Vanier

All I know is that the Eucharist is fundamental for me every day. It has been since I left the Navy, and even before that and this goes back to maybe 70 years ago. The whole mystery of the Eucharist is that Jesus wants to live in me, and me in him. That is the whole sense of Communion. Jesus tells us if we eat his Flesh and drink his Blood, He lives in us and we live in him. The Eucharist is a reality but also a sign that what Jesus wants is to live in me, to live in you and to live in everybody.

It's not just doing things according to the law, it's doing things in order to listen to Jesus. One of the people I love very much is Blessed Cardinal Henry Newman. He talks about the inner voice, listening to conscience. In the Vatican II Council, it says that 'the conscience is the sacred sanctuary where God speaks to every person.'

So, it's about listening to Jesus, taking time. And the Eucharist and Communion – eating the Flesh of Jesus and drinking his Blood – is the sign He wants to live in me and live in people and that we become attentive at each moment to listen to what He wants of us.

We say that 'his will may be done on earth as it is in heaven' but we have to want to do it. So, it's a question of helping Christians to discover that the Eucharist is something extraordinary: where we eat the body of Jesus. It's that incredible, humility of Jesus, Jesus washing our feet. Pope Benedict XVI said, 'A Eucharist that does not flow into the washing of the feet, is a Eucharist that has lost its meaning.' We eat the body of Jesus and drink his blood, so that He lives in us and so we can wash the feet of people – which is to affirm them and to help them grow and to love people. Because people will only know we are Christians by the love we have one for another. It's through love that people know that we're Christians; eating the flesh of Jesus and drinking his blood has gradually a transforming effect. We grow in love. This is the Gospel message; it is what we try to live here in L'Arche all the time. As long as we desire to listen to Jesus and let ourselves be transformed. It's only transformation if we trust the power of the Eucharist. This transformation implies a quality of welcoming the mystery; this is faith and trust. We must be yearning to become like Jesus. It has a transforming effect as long as we open our hearts.

In the book of Revelation (Apocalypse) the Lord says, 'I stand at the door and knock; if somebody hears and opens the door I will come in and eat with that person, I'll become their friend' (Revelation 3:20). Jesus knocks at the door of our hearts with the Eucharist, but we have to open the door then listen to him. That means we don't spend our time getting stressed by doing things. We are people who learn to hear Jesus knocking at the door, and become his friend.

Jean Vanier (Canada) is a philosopher, writer, Religious and moral leader recognised the world over for being the founder of two major international community-based organisations, L'Arche, and Faith and Light, that exist for people with intellectual disabilities. In 2015 Jean was awarded the Templeton Prize. There are to date 151 L'Arche communities over five continents and 1,500 Faith and Light communities in 81 countries which witness to the Gospel, of being living beacons of human transformation.

Healed from Fear

Emily Cavins

I have discovered there is enormous healing power in the Sacrament of the Eucharist. Several years ago, as I found myself tormented by a specific fear, I wondered how I could conquer this fear. I knew that the Eucharist was a sacrament that allows us to partake in the very life of Christ. I was familiar with the words in the Mass, 'Only say the word and I shall be healed' (now 'Only say the word and my soul shall be healed'). I decided these words definitely applied to my situation. During a Mass, as I approached the sacrament, I again prayed for Jesus to heal me. I did not feel anything out of the ordinary at that moment, but after that encounter with the living Christ, I experienced a change. It didn't happen all at once, but nevertheless there was a definite change for the better that continued until I was free of that fear. Many other factors came about in the healing process, but I feel those factors also came from the grace Christ gave me at that moment I received the sacrament. I was healed in much the same way as the centurion's servant in Matthew chapter 8. He received healing by Christ through those same words, 'Only say the word and my servant will be healed.' Those words of faith opened the doors of grace. You too can expectantly approach Jesus with your request for healing and he will answer you.

Emily Cavins (USA) is the author of *My Heart is a Violin: The Autobiography of renowned violinist/composer and Holocaust Survivor Shony Alex Braun*. She is the developer of *Great Adventure Kids* Bible study materials that centre around teaching children the plan of salvation history based on her husband Jeff's *The Great Adventure: A Journey through the Bible*, available at Ascension Press. Emily and her husband Jeff lead Scripture pilgrimages.

The Miracle of the Eucharist

Cardinal Vincent Nichols

Here is a short account of a moment in my life when Our Blessed Lord's presence in the Holy Eucharist came to life for me in a fresh way. Such moments are a great grace, small miracles, given to us for our encouragement and for a deepening of our faith. For me this was certainly a small miracle.

I was with a group of cardinals and bishops in Jerusalem. Preparations had been made for us to celebrate Mass early one morning at the Holy Sepulchre, the very place where Our Lord was buried and from where He rose from the dead.

Those who have been to Jerusalem will know that the space containing the tomb of our Lord is tiny. Only three people can squeeze in. Just outside of it is a small chapel, leading into the tomb itself. That was where our Mass was celebrated, with most of us outside, unable to see inside to the altar itself.

Cardinal Erdo, from Hungry, was celebrant of the Mass. We could hear his words, follow and join in. But we couldn't see. Mass continued just as normal, although at a bit of a distance.

But then came a remarkable moment. We reached that part of the Mass just before Holy Communion – the 'Ecce Agnus Dei' moment – when the priest shows the Sacred Host to the people. This is what happened. Cardinal Erdo bent low and came out of the tomb chapel, suddenly into our sight. There

73

he stood, emerging from the tomb, saying to us all in a loud voice: 'Behold, the Lamb of God who takes away the sins of the world!'

My mind was just flooded! This is what had happened that first Easter morning, in this very place! And now I was there! I was witnessing the Resurrection of the Lord, bursting out of the tomb and coming to me in his victory over death and sin. It was the very place! The very same reality! Jesus, truly present, actually emerging, before my eyes, from the tomb of death to be my Saviour!

Never before had I seen so clearly what is there before us. Yes, we know that at Mass we are present at the foot of the cross as we see Jesus' Body and Blood, given for us, held before us at the Consecration. But this was another precious moment: the Lord coming forth from the place of his death and heralding his life-changing victory! And I was there.

Yes, and I am there every time Mass is celebrated. You are there, every time you are at Mass; there at his tomb; there at his rising from the dead; there to see him emerge from death into life; there to hear the glorious words: 'Behold, the Lamb of God! Behold him who takes away the sins of the world!'

This was my small miracle – to see the Risen Lord emerge from the tomb of his death and come to me, in victory, to draw me to Himself for all time. What a great privilege that was! It stays with me always, now. I hope it is a moment that you too can enter!

Cardinal Vincent Nichols (UK) is the Cardinal of the Catholic Church in England and Wales, Archbishop of Westminster and President of the Catholic Bishops' Conference of England and Wales. He became a Bishop in 1992 and was previously Archbishop of Birmingham for nine years. The Cardinal is the first chancellor of St Mary's University, London, and he is a member of the Santa Marta Group, an alliance endorsed by Pope Francis, set up to help eradicate human trafficking and modern-day slavery around the world.

The Eucharist
Editor

There is a true story that I heard from the times when Russia was under Communist rule. During Mass one Sunday morning armed Communist soldiers burst into a Catholic church, fired their machine guns into the air and announced, 'Anyone here not prepared to die for your faith, leave immediately!' Over the next couple of minutes there was absolute chaos as people scrambled and ran for their lives through various exit points, until eventually there was only a quarter of the original congregation still left in their pews. The soldiers went to the back of the Church, slammed the doors shut, bolted them and proceeded to walk up the aisle with their machine guns in their hands. They got to the altar, turned and faced the congregation, and with tears in their eyes they put down their guns and said, 'What is it, what have you got? We must have that: you were willing to die for it.'

What was it, that if those Catholics had to live without it, they did not want to live at all? What had they discovered in the Mass? What wonder and beauty were they experiencing? There is a phrase that goes 'Unless you've found something worth dying for then you haven't really found anything worth living for.' Like the Catholics in that story, there are people around the world even to this day risking their lives to go to Mass, not knowing if it will be the last thing they will do.

Why? Because they know that when Our Lord Jesus said, 'I am the living bread which came down from heaven; if anyone eats of this bread, he will live for ever' (John 6:51), they knew He meant it!

What impact can the Eucharist make in my life?

In my own life, after an initial conversion through the Sacraments of the Anointing of the Sick and Confession during a bout of depression, I was invited to a retreat where they celebrated Mass. I grew up being told that Christ was truly present in the bread and wine at Mass but I could never truly get my head around that concept – symbolically yes, but really, truly? That would have to be a major miracle that happens every time you go to Mass. But I remember praying and longing to know if Christ was truly present. And on this retreat when I went up to receive Holy Communion, I would describe it like this: it was as if I reached into my chest, pulled out my heart, opened it up and placed a whole load of lit candles in there, closed it up and put it back inside myself. That day my heart felt like it was dancing on fire. And I knew that the words Jesus spoke in John 6 (see above) were true and were real. In the same way, when He promised to feed the five thousand (Matthew 14:13-21) and He did, when He promised to heal blind Bartimaeus (Mark 10:46-52) and He did, when He promised to rise from the dead (Matthew 17:23, Luke 18:33) and He did – and when He promised to be

Then came the day of Unleavened Bread, on which the passover lamb had to be sacrificed. So Jesus sent Peter and John, saying, 'Go and prepare the Passover meal for us, that we may eat it...' They went... and prepared the Passover. And when the hour came, he sat at table, and the apostles with him. And he said to them, 'I have earnestly desired to eat this Passover with you before I suffer; for I tell you I shall not eat it again until it is fulfilled in the Kingdom of God.'...And he took bread, and when he had given thanks he broke it and gave it to them saying, 'This is my body which is given for you. Do this in remembrance of me.' And likewise the cup after supper, saying, 'This cup which is poured out for you is the New Covenant in my blood.'

CCC 1339 (Luke 22:7-20; see Matthew 26:17-29; Mark 14:12-25; 1 Corinthians 11:23-26)

with us until the end of time (Matthew 28:20), I knew that all these promises were fulfilled in Holy Communion at Mass.

I remember one time a comedian friend of mine sent me a text message explaining that his stepdad had been diagnosed with terminal cancer; the doctors had sent him home and said there was no more they could do for him. He asked me if I would pray for his stepdad. I responded by saying I would, but I also had two Holy Masses offered up for him (the greatest prayer we can ever offer up for anybody!). I then contacted him a short time later to enquire about his stepdad. He got back to me to say he could not believe it, but the cancer had completely gone in one of the lungs and it was now possible to operate on the other lung. His stepdad went on to have the operation, to survive, and to have extra quality years of life spent with his family and friends, way past the doctors' expectations. The power of the Mass.

Drawing inspiration from the author Anthony DeStefano, I believe there is one prayer that God can never say 'No' to, and that's when we ask him for spiritual miracles. Think about it, so many seem to ask for temporal things – a bigger car, a nicer house, more popularity and status – yet do so few ask for spiritual blessings that will really change their lives. After all, did not Jesus say, 'How much more will the Heavenly Father give the Holy Spirit to those who ask him?' (Luke 11:13). In

> We break the one bread that provides the medicine of immortality, the antidote for death, and the food that makes us live for ever in Jesus Christ.
>
> *St Ignatius of Antioch*

the times in which we live, the culture can encourage people to be preoccupied with their physical bodies, making sure they have the right healthy diet, getting the right amount of rest, exercising correctly, for a body that will eventually wither and fade, but yet they can neglect their souls which are meant to live for ever.

Christ gives us himself?

Jesus is able to perform great healings through the Eucharist, but the healing starts within our souls. St Thomas Aquinas once stated: 'To receive the Eucharist is to receive Christ himself.' I once heard of a 7-year-old child, after her First Holy Communion, who described her experience as 'receiving a hug from Jesus.' Just as the simplicity of a child's faith takes away the complications of doubts, similarly the great faith of the saints declares with simple trust that God always fulfils his promises. There is a story about St Bonaventure, a wise Doctor of the Church, who was approached by two of his brothers one day. They asked him: 'Bonaventure, how can we be so certain that Jesus Christ is truly present in Holy Communion at Mass?' St Bonaventure looked at them and responded, 'Because He said He would be!' There was a long silence, until eventually they said, 'Is that it?' And he replied, 'That's it.' It was as simple as that.

Imagine if the sun was immediately in front of you at this moment. You would not be able to survive because of its rays, light, power, heat. Yet Scripture tells us all the elements of the universe are subject to Christ (see 1 Corinthians 15:27-28, Ephesians 1:22), so Christ must be even more luminous, bright and powerful. The saints say that because the Lord has regard for our lowliness and weakness He hides himself – conceals himself – in the form of bread in order to enter us both physically and spiritually. If you were God, how else could you come so intimately within your own creation in such a tangible way? And once He is there He is willing to flood our souls with his divinity to sustain us in our lives. As Scott Hahn says, 'When Christ

> Christ's self-offering in the Eucharist... is like inducing nuclear fission in the very heart of being – the victory of love over hatred, the victory of love over death. Only this intimate explosion of good conquering evil can then trigger off the series of transformations that little by little will change the world.
>
> *Pope Emeritus Benedict XVI*

comes at the end of time, He will not have one drop more glory than He has at this moment when we consume all of Him. In the Eucharist we receive what we will be for all eternity.'

There's a story Cardinal Dolan of New York recounts about Archbishop Dominic Tang, a priest in China who spent over 30 years in prison for being nothing other than a Catholic archbishop. After his first five years in solitary confinement he was let out of his cell and granted one request. Think about what you would ask for after so long amidst four walls and such desolation: to phone someone close to you, have a nice meal, get some fresh air? He requested that he wanted to say Mass!

Why did Christ set up the priesthood?

One of the main reasons Christ set up the priesthood was to preserve, maintain and perpetuate his sacrifice at Calvary in the Sacrifice of the Mass. We believe that every time a priest carries out ministry he is 'in persona Christi' – Latin meaning in the person/place of Christ. People such as Archbishop Dominic Tang and all those who make great sacrifices for the Mass, even the ultimate sacrifice, believe the Mass is the greatest event they will ever attend in their lives. Why? Because the Mass is not man-made, it is the work of God himself, as Jesus said, 'Do this in memory of me' (Luke 22:19).

St Pio said, 'Each Holy Mass heard with devotion produces marvellous effects in our souls, spiritual and material graces, that we ourselves do not know. It would be easier for the earth to exist without the sun than without the sacrifice of the Mass.'

Why? Because the Mass is heaven on earth. At every Mass heaven touches down on earth and we enter a heavenly liturgy, a sacred space. If we could see, we would realise that we are joined by the angels and saints.

What's actually happening at Mass?

At Mass, we gather to listen to God's word. The Second Vatican Council describes the Old Testament readings as love letters from God. What He did then, He can do now, so understanding his ways in the past helps us know more fully his ways in the future. A reading from the New Testament helps us grow in our understanding of Christ revealing God's love for us. When the Gospel is read, Christ is present through the priest or deacon 'in persona Christi' proclaiming the Kerygma (Greek word for the proclamation of the Gospel),

> This is the wonderful truth, my dear friends: the Word, which became flesh, two thousand years ago, is present today in the Eucharist.
>
> *St Pope John Paul II*

the Good News; as Pope Francis teaches: 'God loves you, God saves you and God never leaves you.' And as we enter the second part of the Mass that Word of God becomes flesh and we go with him to Calvary, which is fundamentally what the Mass is: the one-time sacrifice of Christ on the cross becomes real and reachable through the miracle of the Mass. The Mass is a re-presentation, that is, a 'making present' of the entire drama of Christ's passion, death and resurrection. As the saints refer to it – 'the unbloody sacrifice of Calvary'.

How is this so? The Mass, an event that happened over 2000 years ago, becomes completely present on our altar because with God there is no time: 'With the Lord, "a day" can mean a thousand years, and a thousand years is like a day' (2 Peter 3:8). God is 'eternal', which means 'the everlasting NOW'. Jesus Christ is both God and man, so as man He died on the Cross for us over 2000 years ago in history (time), but as God He is eternal: in him that historical event is 'now'.

> For as often as you eat this bread and drink the chalice, you proclaim the Lord's death until he comes.
>
> *1 Corinthians 11:26*

And not only that, but when we receive him in Holy Communion, the joy, peace and love we are offered in that moment is a foretaste of the joy, peace and love we will experience in heaven as participants in the resurrection.

In Africa, a missionary priest was once saying Mass at an outpost when, at the end of distribution of Holy Communion, a woman covered in mud crawled up to the sanctuary to receive the Host. Afterwards the rather shocked priest was talking to the sacristan, wondering if the lady was going to do that at every Mass: it was em-barrassing and she was getting mud everywhere. The sacristan looked at him with horror and asked the priest if he had realised that the woman had no feet. She had lost both her feet to gangrene. Crawling to

Mass, which was over a mile away to her, was her only option. The priest felt awful, he got in his car and drove over to see the woman. He explained that she would no longer need to crawl to Mass any more as he was going to arrange for Holy Communion to be brought to her each Sunday. She started to cry and said, 'Please Father, don't take away the privilege it is to crawl to my Saviour.'

That lady knew at Mass she was receiving her Risen Saviour and her sacrifice was minimal. There is not a single saint who ever lived that did not believe Christ was truly present at Holy Communion at Mass. Fr Rainero Cantalamessa (the preacher to the Papal Household) reflected upon the miracle at the Mass when he said, 'The Holy Spirit, who at Easter bursts into the Sepulchre (Tomb), "touches" Christ's body and gives him life again, repeats this wonder in the Eucharist. He comes upon the dead elements of bread and wine and gives them life; He makes them into the Body and Blood of the Redeemer. Truly, as Jesus himself says of the Eucharist, "It is the Spirit that gives life" (John 6:63).'

What is meant to happen when we receive the Body of Christ, the Eucharist?

In my current parish, we run Life Teen Edge nights, a middle school programme to help see young people come closer to God. On one of the nights we held a Eucharistic healing service, after Adoration of the Blessed Sacrament. I went amongst the young people in the chapel with the humeral veil. Based on the woman who touched the hem of Jesus' cloak (Luke 8:43-44) we invited the young people to do the same – to reach out in faith to the Risen Lord. After the service was over one of the teenagers approached me to say that as the Blessed Sacrament was in front of him he heard the words 'Thank you'. This was also confirmed by another young lad separately, who was there. The Eucharist in Greek means 'Thanksgiving'. They would not have known that, but were delighted to hear it when I explained it to them. At Mass the Holy Spirit comes to transform the gifts – bread and wine – then to transform those who receive the gifts! We bring our natural gifts of bread and wine – and the Holy Spirit does the super-natural. St Augustine reflected: '[We] receive the Body of Christ in order to be the Body of Christ.' This sacrament not only conforms us to be more like Christ, living in his power and love, but it unifies us all with one another as brothers and sisters in one Body of Christ.

This unity in the love of God is what attracts others. When we reflect on some of the great sports teams from around the world we realise they need all their members to pull together to be the team they truly can be. This is impossible when key players are missing. It is the same with the Body of Christ. We miss those members who do not play their part, who do not go to Mass, or respond in prayer to God's love, who fail to step up to the plate and be the person God has called them to be with their individual gifts and talents for the Kingdom. And those members of the Body of Christ miss out on union with Jesus through his Church and the Eucharist.

Pope Pius XII said, 'Remember this side of heaven there is no way to come more intimately closer to Jesus than by worthily receiving Him in Holy Communion.' After receiving the Host we are closer than the disciples ever were before Jesus' ascension. The book of Revelation talks about how the Eternal Heavenly banquet, the wedding feast of the Lamb, has begun now… at every Mass. It has started already and we celebrate endlessly the Bridegroom (Christ) to his Bride (his Church) until the day we will all be together to celebrate it in all its fullness and glory.

Is there a condition to the Eucharist working powerfully in my life?

But there is a condition. We must receive Holy Communion worthily. St Paul taught that if our lifestyle contradicts what Jesus taught, we will do more harm than good to ourselves by receiving the Body and Blood of Christ (1 Corinthians 11:27-29). If in any way we are not in communion with the Lord and his Church through breaking any of the Big 'Ten' (Commandments), or not going regularly to Mass, Christ through the Sacrament of the Eucharist will be limited to what He can do in our lives. For example, imagine a plane trying to land on a runway, but the runway is cluttered with large

skips, wheelie bins, rubbish bins, old scrap, disused bricks…
it makes it very difficult for the plane to land smoothly and
safely. The runway must be cleared of all the garbage. We
need to make our interior runways clear of our personal sins
through confession so that the wonder, grace and power of
the Eucharist can do the work God desires within our souls.

Seeing with the eyes of faith?

Will you let him transform your soul to make you more and
more into his image, likeness and holiness through reception
and Adoration of the Eucharist? Mother Teresa (St Teresa of
Kolkata (Calcutta)) knew: 'The time you spend with Jesus
in the Blessed Sacrament is the best time you will spend on
earth. Each moment that you spend with Jesus will deepen
your union with Him and make your soul everlastingly
more beautiful and glorious in heaven and will bring about
everlasting peace on earth.' This is what Jesus meant when
He said that the Kingdom of God is within you!

There is a true story that happened on the 18 August 1996
in Buenos Aries, Argentina. Fr Alejandro Pezet had just
finished distributing Holy Communion when a lady
approached him to tell him that she had found a discarded
Eucharistic host on a candle holder at the back of Church.
The priest went to the back of the Church and he realised the
host was too defiled and badly treated for him to consume it,
so he placed it in a container of water and put it in the

tabernacle. Fr Alejandro came back to it on Monday morning and he saw that the host had been turned into a bloody substance. He reported it to Cardinal Jorge Bergoglio, who, of course, later went on to be Pope Francis. Cardinal Bergoglio had pictures taken which showed a fragment of bloodied flesh that had grown significantly in size. He kept the host in a tabernacle secretly. In 1999 Cardinal Bergoglio had a sample of the bloody fragment taken and sent off to New York to be scientifically analysed. Scientists were not told what it was and this is what they found: the famous cardiologist and forensic pathologist Dr Frederick Zugiba concluded that it was real flesh and blood containing human DNA. It was a fragment of heart muscle responsible for contraction of the heart. The fragment was also inflammatory with a large number of white blood cells, meaning that the heart was alive at the time the sample was taken. It also showed the heart was under severe stress as the owner had been badly beaten about the chest. Wow! That's the heart of the one who has risen and died for you, and a true, authentic Eucharistic miracle, which Pope Francis has spoken about during his Pontificate.

> Every day He humbles Himself just as He did when He came from His heavenly throne into the virgin's womb; every day He comes to us and lets us see Him in lowliness, when He descends from the bosom of the Father into the hands of the priest at the altar.
>
> *St Francis of Assisi*

The Eucharist is spiritual food which helps you live for ever, because it is Christ himself. How do we know that?

Because He said so. He did not lie about his crucifixion, He did not lie about his resurrection, and He did not lie about his ascension, so why would He lie about coming to us as spiritual, sacramental, personal food?

People do not risk their lives for a piece of bread or have their lives transformed by a piece of bread. History, Scripture, the saints have shown God never goes back on his promises. That is why Catholics around the world want to be at Mass and to receive Holy Communion. That is why Catholics around the world are risking their lives to be at Mass: because they know the greatest force both within and outside the universe is present as the Bread of Life. Jesus Christ is the Bread of Life. It is him for sure, because He said it would be, and He is faithful!

I Found What I Was Looking For in a Multitude Whose Median Age Was 78

Paul J. Kim

It was summer break during University. I had recently lost the proverbial tug of war match with the Blessed Mother, due to my serendipitous decision to pick up the Rosary and pray it daily out of some sort of curiosity laced with need. She proceeded to spiritually submit me like a champion mixed martial arts fighter, without even having to lay a finger on me. Strangely, I welcomed her influence because the whole process was marked with a mysterious peace and joy. Like the scene in the Gospel of John during the first miracle of Cana, her gentle yet strong influence was simple: 'Do whatever He (Jesus) tells you.' 'Go to Jesus.' 'Stop staring at me, my child, and go to him already.' I found myself being drawn back to the sacraments... Particularly to the sacrament par excellence: the Eucharist.

It was a weekday... A Monday or Tuesday. The actual day is not so important, but rather the fact that it was a weekday, and not a Sunday. Why? Because there was no obligation whatsoever to attend Mass, and yet my heart was drawn to this weekday Mass like a moth to a flame, like a chubby kid to the last cupcake on the tray, like a young man who was tired of cheap thrills and longing for real promise. I walked into the church, which was marked by a tangible silence and reverence, as the elderly believers (whose median age must have been 78) prepared themselves for the Holy Mass.

I sat in my own vacant pew, made the sign of the cross, and sought to mind my own business. I figured it was better not to make eye contact with old praying ladies who were most likely eyeing me as a potential seminary candidate due to my youthful age and apparent piety. It was more curiosity than piety that led me to the church that day. The bell rang, and the priest began his prayers.

Like thousands of other times in my life, the Mass went on like clockwork, but there was something different about this moment. It wasn't the music, the artwork, or the priest's preaching… It was the openness of my heart, which had been closed and dead-bolted for the majority of my life up until this moment. As the altar was being prepared and the bread and wine offered to God, I listened and stared intently at the prayers, movements, and gestures of the priest. As he uttered the prayer of consecration, 'This is my body, which is given up for you' and lifted up the little host, my eyes met the Lord's, which were hidden beneath the veil of bread. I began to weep silently, not wanting to draw attention to myself.

Like so many chance encounters throughout the Gospel, I, like Zacchaeus, sat in the tree while the Lord walked by. The Lord looked into my eyes, and surgically into my soul, and despite all that was broken in me due to sin… He nonetheless invited me to be in friendship with him. I responded with a yes, because his approach was so loving, merciful, kind, and real. Ironically, He had been inviting me for years, but I just wasn't interested or convinced. I finally accepted the grace to believe that Jesus Christ was truly present: body, blood, soul, and divinity, in the Most Blessed Sacrament. And from that moment on, my experience of every Mass was no longer an obligation, but rather an opportunity to witness and partake in a miracle. What a gift: that God himself, whom the universe cannot contain, would humble himself into the form of a slave. No, even more than that. He would become our very food and nourishment as we walk through the exodus of our human experience towards the promised land of everlasting life.

Every sanctuary candle, is now a porch light that our Heavenly Father leaves on for me, so that I can come with confidence at any time towards his home: the tabernacle in every Catholic Church throughout the world. The invitation is always there, where He waits for you and me. Where we can come as we are, and visit any time and love and be loved by the One Who loved us first.

Paul J. Kim (USA) is an international speaker and musician who combines both ministries in his unique way of evangelising and teaching. He has released two albums *The World Sings* and *Run Fly Fall* with original songs and covers available at – PJKmusic.com. His vocal abilities also include beat-boxing (vocal drumming), harmonies and lyrics.

Transformed by Love
David Wells

The miracle of the Eucharist comes most naturally to those who enter into it with humility. We approach it somewhat foolishly, recognising that there is always something greater here than we can first know or understand. You don't have to be learned or deep in the conventional sense to get it. The miracle isn't about what we do. It is about what God does.

The switching off of self isn't a docile stupid act. Our intellectual critique is an important gift. Yet, if God comes to us as an idea to be understood then the Eucharist is constrained by human capacity, our reason, our ego and our imagination. If God offers himself not as information but as nourishment, then those capacities become less reliable. It would be folly to believe that this can be grasped within our physical concrete existence. Before this mystical unfathomable realm, I am humbled away from my abilities.

So how does the sacrament begin to manifest itself in something we might call a miracle?

The miracle is of transformation. How can something which starts as one thing, become completely something else? I'm standing in the loft of a large church among a congregation of mainly African people. During the opening prayer, my mind has wondered away from my surroundings. I'm distracted by the barrage of anxieties I unconsciously brought with me. A time of reflection is lost to temporal uncertainties: my performance at work, my children's welfare, untidy relationships, so many unfinished tasks I have to complete. It's a tumble of issues rotating round, one upon another, intruding like a thief into my private space.

There is something extravagant about the way African communities offer bread and wine at the offertory. The baskets carrying these gifts were unfamiliarly huge. In my experience, the bread and wine is usually presented on discrete little silver plates and in small glass decanters. This, though, was colourful and flamboyant. The baskets were decorated, large and lavish. The wine in large earthenware urns. As the gifts of bread and wine were processed from the back of the Church, I was confronted by a thought which felt foreign to me: *'Put your life in the basket.'* Because they were large baskets, the thought seemed strangely reasonable to me as if such a thing could be quantified by size. As the priest received the gifts at the altar I saw with fresh clarity my life set inside another context. Jesus didn't come to transform the neat and tidy. My folly and fear, my hopes and ambitions, all my untrained and undisciplined thoughts were sitting there on the altar. This humble and imperfect offering of bread and wine is also the sum total of our limited achievements. My bruised and hurting little life is being transformed. All I had to do was put it in the basket.

Observing people processing up to receive the Eucharist, I encounter a second miracle: that for all our limitations we can receive what is transformed. The man bent over his walking stick, the mother carrying her little girl, the tall young man in bright yellow jeans. They have discovered something. We are going forward together each in our own way bruised, hurting and dirty, to receive what is perfect. God enters in. All I have to do now is take, eat and drink.

I'd like to say at this point that my worries flittered away like butterflies and that I left church resolved to live perfectly. Such aspirations barely make it to the car park. That wasn't the miracle. The miracle is that we'll all be back again, because the transforming love of God keeps putting us back together when we can't mend ourselves. We receive the Lamb of God, who takes away the sins of the world and we are happy to be called to this supper.

David Wells (UK) is an international speaker, catechist and author of two books: *The Reluctant Disciple* and *The Grateful Disciple* both available from Redemptorist Publications. He was the former Director of Adult Formation and Youth Ministry for the Diocese of Plymouth. David continues to support his Diocese in assisting schools in their contribution to the New Evangelisation.

The High Priest's Promise for a Dying Man

Fr Leo E. Patalinghug IVDei

It was a busy day, typical for a young associate pastor trying to save the world. I was leaving from the hospital for my second call that day when I received yet another call to visit an elderly man in the nursing home. He was actively dying. His children were called to be with him in his last hours, or days. No one, but God, really knows those details.

I sprang into action, perhaps a bit too quickly – as a young enthusiastic priest. I called the family, all waiting at the bedside of their beloved father. I asked if he could receive Communion. They said they didn't know if he could swallow the Host. I should have presumed being prepared for Viaticum, just in case. But, being a bit too hasty, I didn't stop by the parish to obtain a reserved consecrated Host.

When I got to the nursing home, I met the charge nurse, a faithful parishioner. She knew and told me, 'Mr John was a very faithful parishioner who loved receiving the Eucharist. You can give him a very small piece and I'll melt ice to dissolve it so that he swallows it.'

I immediately felt bad for not bringing Holy Communion. I would have returned to the church to bring back Communion, but the family immediately invited me to the room for the anointing prayers. They were anxious too.

At the conclusion of the prayers, the dad was still unresponsive. I thought to myself, 'Maybe it was best not to bring Viaticum as he wouldn't know either way.' So, after a few consoling words, and before I was ready to depart, I invited the family to say an extra set of our Catholic 'Traditional-Trio' of prayers: the Our Father, Hail Mary and Glory Be. To our surprise, the father opened his eyes, looked at me and started to mouth the words slowly. I, myself, and the family around the bedside were shocked. We slowed down so that he could lead us (myself included) in the prayers. It was very touching indeed.

At the end of the prayers however, something strange happened. His eyes gazed upward, beyond us all. He then strained his neck and silently mouthed the word 'Amen'. He proceeded to open his mouth, put out his tongue, gently closed his mouth. He serenely closed his eyes and he softly began to chew. He then obviously swallowed 'something' satisfying because the look on his face was so serene.

I was shocked. My thoughts raced. 'Did he just receive Viaticum – Holy Communion? What was he chewing? Why did he say, "Amen" and look like he received Communion on the tongue? Did I just see a miracle? Did Jesus, the High Priest give this man what I could not give him?'

I didn't see a mystical host, but we certainly witnessed something miraculous: an unresponsive dying man 'received' what appeared to be an invisible Holy Communion as

Viaticum, more likely at the hands of the Divine Physician. We saw him chew and swallow something. We saw his peaceful expression, a definite sign that God was with him. After all, the word 'viaticum' simply means, *on the way with you*, to describe how the Eucharist, our Last Supper is the Food on our journey to heaven. So, while I didn't bring Viaticum, that didn't stop God from accompanying this faithful man to everlasting life.

This experience, one that I will never forget, reminded me of how God can work through my limitations as a priest – even a young priest with boundless energy. My intention was good, my pastoral skills developing, and my desire to respond quickly was noble. But despite all of that, I wasn't prepared and didn't bring Holy Communion – something Mr John would have wanted. But, God answered his prayers, no thanks to me. Let's just say I'm grateful for my happy fault. It gave me a chance to experience something miraculous and to strengthen my faith that God is the one who initiates and completes the sacramental grace – even through the limitations of the priest.

This holy man died later that day. His family requested that I tell that story at the funeral homily. People received Communion in a more solemn fashion that day.

Viaticum *is* real. God *is* with us on our way to heaven. We can call it 'miraculous' that God would be so intimately united with us in our last days on earth to eternity. Or, we can just call it 'faith'.

Fr Leo E. Patalinghug (Philippines/USA) is a priest member of the community of consecrated life, Voluntas Dei (The Will of God). He is an international Author, Speaker, TV & Radio Host, and Founder of GraceBeforeMeals.com an international apostolate to help strengthen families and relationship through God's gift of a family meal and TheTableFoundation.org with the mission to elevate culture and family life, one meal at a time.

In that little host is the solution to all the problems of the world.

St Pope John Paull II

For I received from the Lord what I also delivered to you, that the Lord Jesus on the night when he was betrayed took bread, and when he had given thanks, he broke it, and said, 'This is my body, which is for you. Do this in remembrance of me.' In the same way also the chalice, after supper, saying, 'This chalice is the new covenant in my blood. Do this, as often as you drink it, in remembrance of me.'

1 Corinthians 11:23-25

There is no more effective way of drawing down God's blessing on a sinful, hungry, needy, wandering and confused world than by praying for others in Mass and through Mass.

Fr J. A. Hardon

THE SACRAMENT OF BAPTISM

Today your offences are blotted out and your names are written down. The priests blot out in the water, and Christ writes down in heaven.

St Ephraem the Syrian

We were buried therefore with him by baptism into death, so that as Christ was raised from the dead by the glory of the Father, we too might walk in newness of life.

Romans 6:4

And if [we are] children, then heirs, heirs of God and fellow heirs with Christ.

Romans 8:17

The Big 'YES'

David Payne

I've been back in the Church as a committed Christian for nearly 30 years now. That may not sound very significant in itself but when I'm reminded of this, it never ceases to amaze me! At 25 I was a burnt-out drug-addicted hopeless young man heading for an early grave and yet it all turned around for me when I heard an ex-Hells Angel preach the amazing news that Jesus is alive today and can restore even the most broken soul.

I was brought up as a Catholic but at 14 I'd had enough! It all seemed very boring and mostly untrue so I stopped going to Mass and planned to run my life without the need of stuffy religion. It didn't take long for things to start falling apart. By 15, I was experiencing much inner turmoil and emptiness and consequently began to get into serious trouble at school. At 16 I became a punk rocker and started messing with a lot of different drugs. Things were looking very bleak indeed.

Two years later my life took a major turn when I got involved in a serious relationship which motivated me to make some radical changes. I set out to make money thinking that would solve all my problems! I was soon running my own company in the City of London, living with my girlfriend in a posh Hampstead apartment and driving a flashy Italian sports car. Everything looked good, at least on the outside! However, the inner emptiness hadn't been filled and within a few years my life totally imploded. The girl left me, the business folded and the car blew up. My fragile empire had collapsed and stupidly I turned to hard drugs to numb my extreme inner pain. It began a very dark and dangerous few years of my life that would head towards a very nasty conclusion.

Thankfully, this isn't the end of the story because my good old Catholic mother was praying for me! I discovered that a mother's prayers are incredibly potent and after many years of battling for her broken son, her prayers were answered. After a very scary experience of evil whilst on LSD, I agreed, in my desperation, to go to hear the Hells Angel speak about his faith. Despite a lot of anxiety and scepticism, I found him absolutely captivating. His story was far more extreme than mine and yet he'd found the peace and meaning that I desperately craved for. He told us how – it was all because of Jesus Christ!

He spoke about Jesus in a way I'd never heard before. Jesus was a fairy tale to me or, at best, a historical figure like Queen Victoria but this awesome-looking preacher spoke about Jesus like he knew him personally, as if he was his best friend. He told us that what Jesus had done 2000 years ago, 2000 miles away was like the releasing of nuclear-like power on this planet and that power, he said, is still flowing today and can fill, heal, restore and rejuvenate any life, however broken or dysfunctional it may be. This really was 'good news' to my ears!

It got even better when he told us that this amazing offer of new life is totally *free*, you don't have to pay for it or earn it with good behaviour. It's not just for the respectable or holy, you don't need to clean yourself up before Jesus will fill you with his life-giving presence... it's absolutely unconditional. All we need to do is say 'YES' in our hearts. 'Yes' to his presence, 'Yes' to his healing forgiveness and 'Yes' to becoming a disciple, a follower of Jesus.

I realised that I'd never done that, despite the years of going to church week after week. So, with my heart pounding, I stood to my feet in the midst of the crowded hall and prayed the biggest prayer of my life. I surrendered my whole, broken, limping life to Jesus; I said 'Yes' to everything He had for me and asked for his healing forgiveness to start flowing in my heart.

To my relief (and the great relief of my mum!) I discovered it's absolutely true – Jesus is alive! Almost immediately I felt an inner peace begin to flow in my heart, and hope and joy as well. I soon went to a priest for the Sacrament of Reconciliation. It had been a long time since I'd confessed my sins and I had a very lengthy list! When I left, I truly felt clean on the inside for the first time in years.

The Hells Angel was right – when you say 'Yes' to Jesus then his new life really does fill and restore us. I now know that every Catholic is called to say this 'Yes' to the great gift of our baptism that many of us received as babies. Baptism is the most powerful gift that opens us to the fullness of Christ. But it's not magic: the Church tells us that we need to 'activate' it with faith as adults. When we do, our lives are transformed in so many different ways.

David Payne (UK) is a speaker and the Director of CaFE, a charity producing films for parishes and schools. He speaks at conferences and leads retreats in the UK and is also the author of four books including *ALIVE* which is an easy-to-read account of his conversion and life in the Church. Available from www.faithcafe.org.

Power of Baptism Shining Through

Carolyne D'cruze

I have been a catechist for the RCIA in my parish for about 17 years. I find it a great privilege to be able to share the beauty and wisdom of the teachings of the Catholic Church I love with adults who are spiritually searching in their lives.

In our parish, we currently use a mixture of teaching on an article of faith or tradition of the Church, which is given by the parish priest, and on alternative weeks, a lectionary-based catechesis, which I lead, and which is based on the Sunday Mass readings. In this, participants are encouraged to share how the readings speak to their own personal lives and the world around them. I'm often really inspired by the insights they share.

I have always believed in the power of baptism as 'God's most beautiful and magnificent gift' (St Gregory of Nazianzus), but in recent years this has grown stronger. The *Catechism of the Catholic Church* states that baptism is 'the sacrament of **regeneration** through water in the word' and that 'the baptised becomes a **new creation**' (CCC 1213). And I believe that I have literally seen this happen as I have witnessed the newly baptised often looking somehow physically different after receiving the sacrament. It is as if the grace of this sacrament starts to shine through them so strongly that it can be physically seen and I have noticed a radiance and a light shining through them. I remember the radiance of a woman following her baptism a few years ago, and remarking to her in the following weeks that she looked different, that she was 'lit up'. She told me that a family member had said the same thing to her, and also some work colleagues, who were not even aware that she had just been baptised.

Last year a mother and son were baptised at the Easter Vigil. At the time of the baptism when the water was being poured over the little boy's head he was very calm and joyful. I noticed that when his mother was baptised, she winced as the water was poured over her head. When I spoke to her afterwards about this she said she couldn't help wincing because the water was freezing. Yet her little son said that he hadn't found the water cold at all. What was happening there, I wondered? Both of them looked so radiant and exuded so much joy, which is exactly as it should be because baptism is the beginning of new life. The little boy had sat through a two-and-a-half-hour Easter Vigil service and told me excitedly afterwards that he wanted to do it all over again – and this from a child who was usually restless during a 45-minute Sunday Mass!

I have been hearing again and again how the reception of the sacraments is changing people's lives. One man who was received into the Church a few years ago told me that the Mass had come alive for him, whereas previously he had only gone to accompany his children. Another told me that he is experiencing the love of God in a very personal way and that he knows he is a child of God. He has been profoundly touched by the reception of the sacraments. Another has told me that she wants to be a 'better person' now and that her life is changing for the better. I should not be surprised by any of this as Jesus is now living inside these people in a new way. I firmly believe that the radiance that the newly received exude gives truth to the interior transformation occurring within and that they are being changed from the inside out.

Carolyne D'cruze (UK) is a Practice Manager for a Consultant Dermatologist. She has been a Catechist for RCIA for over 17 years and is a speaker for Catholic Voices. She also coordinates a weekly Catholic Charismatic prayer group.

What Is God's Plan for Me?

Michael Dopp

I was 38 but unsure of many things. I didn't know what to make of St Boniface Catholic Church in Maryhill. While it was not my first time there, it was still new to me. The soaring ceilings, the deep red carpet, and the phenomenal high altar that held the remarkable statues of Jesus flanked by John the Evangelist and St Boniface – all inspired curiosity and awe.

Maryhill came about its name honestly. It is a village with deep German Catholic roots and so, when being renamed, the priest suggested it include the name of Mary. It is also a village with a striking hill on which sits the church. Thus these two characteristics were united to form the name of Maryhill. The parish was named after St Boniface, the tremendous missionary to Germany, who is remembered for cutting down a tree that was considered sacred by some Germanic pagans and building a Catholic Church out of it. He could wield both a Bible and an axe in his quest to become holy and to evangelise.

Many a tree was cut down to build St Boniface Church as it is a large and prominent building with a soaring steeple and magnificent stained glass. It was a suitable church as its size and presence echo the significant and vital change that was to happen to the trajectory of my life that day.

My family – immediate and extended – gathered near the front although I was not sure why. I found out soon enough when, without warning, Fr Sherlock poured water upon my head and said. 'I baptise you in the name of the Father, and of the Son, and of the Holy Spirit.' I don't remember him saying these words, likely because I was only 38 days old. But I do know that he did say them, just as I know that those powerful words, prayed at the command of Christ, have welcomed the multitudes of the centuries into the Church.

It was the greatest day of my life. Yes. THE GREATEST. Born in the state of original sin and separation from God, my soul had been washed and cleansed. I was no longer in bondage to sin, but now enjoyed the freedom of a son of God. I became his child. The seed of grace that will grow, I hope, into the oak of glory was planted within me. I experienced the dying and rising with Christ of which Paul speaks. Where there was darkness in my soul, Christ brought his light. Where there was bondage, Christ brought freedom. Where there were the seeds of despair, Christ brought hope. And where there was a vacancy, God himself came to dwell. On 19 August 1979, I entered the Church. Like billions before me, my life was given a decisive shape and specific direction. I could echo the words of the martyrs in the moments before their death: I am a Christian.

But something else happened that day. I was given, in baptism, two missions: to be a saint and to be a missionary. I'll be straight with you, the call to heroic virtue/the perfection of charity/transforming union AND the call to share the Gospel of Jesus Christ with others – this can seem like quite a bit for a 38-day-old. I was just trying to not get spit up on my white gown and to figure out how to use my fingers. Now I also had to be a saint and a missionary?

So here I am today. Still 38 but now years old rather than days old. Much has changed of course, but two fundamental truths remain as anchors for everything: I am still called to be a saint and I am still called to be a missionary. Now Christ, in his mercy, journeys with me in this. He feeds me with his sacraments, encourages me in prayer, and speaks in the silence of my heart. But since there is no specific and exact roadmap, the path I (and all of us) have taken has turns, valleys, detours, U-turns, potholes, red lights, breakdowns, oil leaks, empty tanks, and flat tires while also having gorgeous vistas, soaring mountains, quiet plains, bridges, and open roads. And what it has at the end of this long and singular path is simply him. God. He who came into my soul at baptism, awaits me at the destination. He first came to live in me and to reveal to me his love. Now He invites me to heaven, where there is not a baptism but a marriage – the bridegroom and his Church. And He calls me to enter fully into this heavenly marriage now (holiness). But He also gives me the immense privilege of inviting others to this wedding feast (mission).

My life is ordered by, and to, these two vocations. It hasn't always worked out well. I am still far from the heights of holiness. And if I am poor at being a saint, I'm even poorer at being a missionary. Fear, pride, laziness, and a host of other sins and defects hold me back from being the missionary I am called to be. But Christ is patient. While He does not delight in my mediocrity, He sticks with me and continues to call me forth. His mercy is always available. He beckons me forward reminding me that He will never ever ever give up on me.

And in my heart I do desire to respond. At times I feel like a pilgrim moving to the distant peak of a mountain. Up and down I go, climbing in heat and cold, going left, going right, trying to go straight. Then on occasions looking up. Sometimes it seems like the distant peak is not quite so distant. Sometimes it seems the distant peak is VERY distant. But one thing that cannot be denied – when I look behind I see the hills and valleys, rivers and meadows, the forests and fields that his grace has allowed me to cross.

God has brought me to a new place in these 38 years. I have grown a little in virtue, I am learning to pray, I try to evangelise. And anytime that I am off course, when the things of this world or the promises of the flesh or the lies of the devil ring in my ears, I can always be reminded of what God whispered to me at baptism: I was his son and by adoption, I was called to partake in his very life. This reorients my life.

It reminds me and redirects me. It calls me back when I have wandered. But it also fills my heart with immense joy for the path to the peak is a good path to a good peak.

It is a strange thing to peg an unremembered day as the greatest. Our baptism (as infants) has none of the nervousness of our first confession, excitement of our First Communion, anticipation of our confirmation, or outward celebrations of our wedding. It is a day like Nazareth – small, hidden, almost forgettable. Yet it is the day that really matters, for in it God gives us his dream for our life. So next time you wonder, 'What is God's plan for me?' remember that He told you already, sometime around when you were 38.

Michael Dopp (Canada) is the founder of the Mission of the Redeemer Ministries, The New Evangelization Summit and Relit, ministries that are involved and dedicated to the New Evangelisation and training people up in evangelisation skills. Michael's ministry of speaking and teaching has taken him to evangelisation and mission projects in Europe, Africa, and North America.

Baptism
Editor with Barbara Reed Mason

Months after I got my appointment as a hospital chaplain I was saying Mass one Wednesday afternoon when I realised I did not have a Mass intention for that day. I asked Our Lady what her Son wanted me to pray for and felt a deep impulse within my heart to pray for 'Miracles'. So I did. About four hours later the emergency hospital pager went off, which generally means that someone is dying and in great need of a priest. Arriving at the ward, I greeted the nurse who brought me into a side room where a middle-aged man was sitting up in bed. He looked very ill and had a sadness about him.

I asked, 'Is everything okay?'

He said, 'No, I'm dying Father and I've never been baptised.' He said, 'Will you baptise me?'

It was a great honour that day not only to baptise him, but to confirm him and give him his First Holy Communion. His sister and mother stood at my side, their eyes streaming with tears. At the end of it, I noticed he had a great joy and peace about him. He was changed, transformed, as something amazing had happened to him: he was born into new life.

Have you ever wished you had somebody else's life? Maybe you wanted their job, their car, their wealth, their opportunities…their life (I've always wanted to be a parish priest in Barbados or Real Madrid's chaplain). But what if you were offered something far greater? What about instead of having someone else's life you had God's life: his very being, very existence? Well, here's the good news: if you're baptised – you do! If you're not – you're welcome to have it! Through baptism, God literally gives his whole self, his Life and love to you. Wow! Can you handle this truth?!! Baptism is not just about having your sins washed away, but becoming part of God's royal family, his divine offspring, adopted as his son or daughter – you're in the inheritance plan. By nature, Jesus is his son, but we become his children through baptism into Jesus Christ.

> What have I done with my baptism and confirmation? Is Christ really at the centre of my life? Do I have time for prayer in my life? Do I live my life as a vocation and mission?
>
> *St Pope John Paul II*

Sacraments

My Diocesan brother Fr Gerrard Barry says, 'Every time a sacrament is celebrated "heaven opens".' In baptism the Holy Spirit of God bursts into your life, his love is poured into our hearts. We are transformed – we now share his Divine nature. Comic book/movie superheroes have nothing on those of us who are baptised! So here is an example of what I'm trying to say: it is a bit basic, but just use your imagination. Imagine having a large glass jug full of water in front of you with an empty glass next to it. The glass jug represents God (stay with me) and the glass is someone before baptism.

We are made in God's image and likeness but we are empty vessels needing the power of God's love. At baptism God empties himself out into us with his life and love (pouring the water from the jug into the glass – to halfway). God's love has a name: the Holy Spirit. But the glass is not yet full because God's life in us needs to be practised in a living, real relationship with him and with others, otherwise this life within us remains dormant. It needs to be activated and filled up time and time again by practising our faith and receiving more of God's love and power by going to Mass, confession, reading Scripture, praying, and so on.

However, human nature is weak. There are holes at the bottom of the glass where it leaks, since we are sinful and battle with our brokenness. Therefore, the glass needs a constant outpouring from the jug, perpetually filled up to make up for the leaks (our sin and faults). It needs to be overflowing, and if it is, other lives will be impacted and attracted to that God-powered/love-filled life

> Therefore if anyone is in Christ, he is a new creation; the old has passed away, behold, the new has come.
>
> *2 Corinthians 5:17*

– think of empty glasses being underneath a glass that is spilling over – alternatively think of someone standing underneath a waterfall, constantly being filled and overflowing despite losing any water. Baptism is meant to change us, to transform us as it did that hospital patient, as our very nature is elevated by sharing in God's love, divinity

117

and holiness. Early friends of Jesus noted this. St Peter says we have become partakers/sharers of the divine nature (2 Peter 1:4) and the radically converted St Paul tells us we are temples of the Holy Spirit. This is the ultimate makeover, as we are recreated, reborn, made new, supernaturally transformed into adopted sons and daughters of God! That's why we now call him 'Dad', 'Abba, Father' (Romans 8:15), because we are not strangers, lodgers or visitors but his children.

A friend of mine was talking to a 13-year-old lad a short time back about baptism. He was quite obstinate because he had not been baptised, and when my friend encouraged him to receive the Sacrament of Baptism, he asked, 'What difference will it make?' I guess he had come across too many examples of people who were baptised who have not let God's Spirit change their life.

Why does someone need to be baptised?

In the beginning of time no one needed to be baptised. That is when God first created Man (that is, human beings: male and female) in his image and likeness. Why did he do that? God wanted to share his life and give his children dominion over all creation (see Genesis 1:26-28). Man was created to be in intimate union with God who is Love, Wisdom, and Eternal Life. Man had it all! Man was holy because the Holy Spirit of God lived in him (and her!). God created the first human beings to live for ever (see Wisdom 2:23), and as long as they remained in God they would never have to suffer or die. How could that be? Because they were joined with Eternal Life himself.

But something dreadful happened. Some other creatures of God called angels (who were pure spirits) rebelled against him because they discovered He was choosing 'lesser' creatures than themselves to be his sons and daughters: creatures who were both spirit and body. The archangel Lucifer was their leader, who then became known as Satan or the devil. He decided to try to mess up God's plan, so he sneaked up on our first parents and convinced them to separate themselves from God. He got them to believe that they could be like God without him. By choosing to believe his lie they gave the devil their allegiance instead of their Father-God. From that time onwards the devil had a certain dominion over them (CCC 407). Death entered human history because humankind separated from Eternal Life. Sin, as we know, is separation from God. All human beings afterwards were born in this condition of 'death of the soul' and its consequences.

> Where is your baptism? You are baptised in your professions, in the fields of workers, in the market. Wherever there is someone who has been baptised, that is where the Church is. There is a prophet there. Let us not hide the talent that God gave us on the day of our baptism and let us truly live the beauty and responsibility of being a prophetic people.
>
> *Blessed Oscar Romero*

The rescue operation

The human race needed to be rescued from an impossible situation, but how? A number of years ago I recall hearing about a tragic boating/ferry disaster. The dock doors of the ferry had not been closed and water started to rush in as the ferry began its journey. Within a couple of minutes the ferry was capsizing and sinking. As tragedy and chaos ensued, on board the vessel there was a group of passengers trapped who could not make it to safety because of a large gap with a huge drop. However, there was a man who was over six foot who put his feet and his arms between two metal railings either side of the gap and made himself a human bridge where people could crawl across him to safety. He saved over 22 people that day. What a heroic feat! But that's exactly what Jesus did for everybody: He created a bridge from earth to heaven. Let me explain:

A sin (even if it's small) against an eternal/infinite being demanded an eternal/infinite atonement (making up for). You see, God is all-loving and merciful but He is also all-just.

> When we welcome the Holy Spirit in our hearts, Christ Himself becomes present in us and takes form in our lives. Through us and our actions, it will be He who prays and forgives, gives hope and consolation, serves our brothers, helps those in need and helps spread communion and peace.
>
> *Pope Francis*

What Jesus did for us

As we said earlier, there was a point in history when death was the end. That was natural because the penalty of sin was death. But then came Jesus, the king of the supernatural. Jesus smashed death for ever. Jesus stared death in the face and beat it back. He came for one reason, to take upon himself our sin and shame and to die with it... to nail our sins, our brokenness to the cross and die with all that once and for all so we would not have to experience eternal death. But because He was God as well as man, death couldn't hold him back, and so, on the third day He rose again and ascended into heaven in order to set up a pathway, a bridge from earth to heaven. For all those baptised into him – from the moment He sent his Spirit at Pentecost into the hearts and souls of his apostles, and continuing through generations since – and for all those who follow him and live by his teachings, physical death is not the end, but merely a change of address to eternal life in God. As St Irenaeus expressed, 'God became man so we could become God.'

> Baptism is the way out of the Kingdom of death into life, the gateway to the Church, and the beginning of a lasting communion with God.
>
> *YouCat, 194 [1213-1216, 1276-1278]*

And so, in the dark trenches and battlefields of our own sin there is an invitation to be baptised into Christ, taking on his identity and image becoming a member of his Body, the Church. As the Anglican Bishop Tom Wright reflected (*Mark: For Everyone Bible Studies*):

> When the living God looks at us, at every baptised and believing Christian, he says to us what he said to Jesus on that day [at the River Jordan]. He sees us, not as we are in ourselves, but as we are in Jesus Christ… God looks at us, and says, 'You are my dear, dear child; I'm delighted with you.'

We share in the same Spirit that Christ had when He walked this earth, no less, no different, so all the same supernatural potential is within us, especially to love as Christ did. Pope Francis says, 'We are called to live our baptism every day as an actual reality in our existence.' One example of the gifts from baptism is to love with the very love of God.

Why baptise babies?

A good question!

Babies are not capable of looking after themselves and providing for their own needs, so the parents have to make all the decisions for them in love, i.e. when they are crying, parents pick them up and feed them; parents look after them when they need changing, or when they are sick and need medicine and so on. But is there any greater decision the parents can make than to have their child baptised? Bearing in mind what you have read above, of primary importance for the parents is to provide for their children spiritually. As *YouCat*, 197 teaches, just as every person is born with the ability to speak but must learn a language, so too every person is born with the ability to believe. However, they must be familiar with the faith and grow up in a faith environment. As the child matures he or she will have to make a decision for this faith and personally say 'Yes' to Jesus, particularly through the Sacrament of Confirmation.

Ongoing conversion

Bishop Robert Barron talks about how the Holy Spirit draws us up out of this fallen world into a new world, into the very life of God, the Trinity. As the *Catechism* says: 'God himself is an eternal exchange of love, Father, Son and Spirit, and he has destined us to share in that exchange' (CCC 221). That is why baptism lifts us up, saves us, enlightens and transforms us: we are

> He desires all men to be saved and to come to the knowledge of the truth.
>
> *1 Timothy 2:4*

born again as new creations in Christ. Baptised in the Holy Spirit, our souls are immersed in the ocean of Divine love.

However, baptism isn't the end but rather the beginning of new life in Christ. There is constantly more for us, but thankfully we are not left on our own in this time of growth in the spirit. God wants us to become more like his Son, so He gives us supernatural gifts and graces in the sacraments to help us live our vocation of 'new life in the Holy Spirit'. But it is up to us to continually choose to follow God's plan or our own plan. Sin still can get in the way, and weaken or even block the new spiritual life. This is why the Lord gave us the Sacrament of Reconciliation (confession).

The Gateway to Life in the Spirit
Michelle Moran

I grew up in a not very religious but loving and secure family. At the age of 16 my spiritual eyes were opened when I met members of a religious sect on the street in my home city. Thankfully, after this awakening, my search (or the Holy Spirit) led me to encountering the Lord in a personal way at a summer camp run by the SVP. It was the early days of the Catholic Charismatic Renewal and many of the leaders at the camp were 'on fire' with the love of God. Their witness spoke so powerfully to me and I knew that I wanted whatever they had. So, to my surprise, at the end of my time at the camp, I found myself responding to an invitation to be prayed with. When I was asked what I wanted to receive from the Lord, my reply was 'everything'. The Lord always takes us at our word, so that initial conversion, which obviously needed to deepen and mature, has led me on a path whereby I have been a fulltime missionary for more than 30 years.

After the experience at the camp, I needed to enter into the community of the Church and it was a surprise for me to discover that I had been baptised as a baby and that baptism meant I was already part of the community. This was like encountering a previously undiscovered family; I now had a new sense of belonging. I learned that in baptism we are washed in the waters of regeneration and we are born anew.

This is exactly what I had experienced at the camp. My life had been transformed and I now had a clear identity. I seemed to have more purpose and direction. Subsequently, I discovered that baptism is the most fundamental sacrament. It is the basis of the Christian life, the gateway to life in the Spirit and shared by all who call themselves Christian.

Over time I have come to see that baptism isn't just something done to us as infants. It is a stream of grace for daily living. In baptism, all the faithful are anointed as priests, prophets and kings. This anointing, together with confirmation, empowers me and all the people of God, for ministry. I take my place alongside my brothers and sisters as part of the common priesthood, praying for the world. Baptismal grace helps us to radiate the love of God which has been poured into our hearts by the Holy Spirit (Romans 5:5). This profound witness of love can transform the world. Drawing upon the prophetic anointing of baptism enables me to trust in the Lord and find my voice, to not be afraid to speak words of truth and life. Sharing in Christ's kingship reminds me that I have a dignity and a role and responsibility within the body of Christ. However, Christ's kingship was not of this world. The call is to humble submission and to continue to embrace my baptism through dying to self in order to rise to new life. Undoubtedly, drawing upon my baptismal grace has been the bedrock and sustenance of my particular missionary calling over the past 30 years.

Michelle Moran (UK), together with her husband Peter, is a founder member of Sion Catholic Community for Evangelism in the UK. She has been engaged internationally in evangelism and mission fulltime for the past 30 years and has authored several books and articles about evangelisation. She is the former President of the International Catholic Charismatic Renewal Services, based in the Vatican and she has been a member of the Pontifical Council for the Laity since 2008.

Plunged into New Life

Hannah Hayward

Baptism is best described, I think, as a kind of spiritual 'bath'. In fact, the word 'baptise' comes from the Greek word baptizein which means 'to plunge' or 'immerse'. The Church tells us that baptism is a sort of 'plunging' into Christ's burial and death, and a 'rising again' with Christ out of the grave into a 'new life'. This spiritual plunging is symbolised through three immersions (or pouring) of water. I may not have appreciated this apparently random soaking as a baby on the day of my baptism. However, now I understand what it is to be truly clean, I am so grateful to my parents for ensuring I had a good wash, both spiritual and physical! In fact, the *Catechism of the Catholic Church* says that, at my baptism, I was 'freed from the power of darkness and brought into the realm of the freedom of the children of God' (CCC 1250). I love that description. What a wash!

However, I must admit, I can look at my own *spiritual* life and wonder 'Where did that purity go?' Where has that 'baptismal grace' gone in me? In baptism I know I was washed clean, I was filled with the life of Christ; but where has that life gone now? The answer, of course, is *nowhere*! I will always be baptised. It is not possible to be *un*baptised. The grace remains with me (unless I willingly sever myself completely from it through mortal sin). I am a child of God.

Always. Unfortunately, the effects of sin remain, and I choose to reject this innate goodness, and bathe in the muddy waters of self-determination, power-wielding, pride and greed. My 'grown-up' independence from God leads me away from his Fatherhood, and into all kinds of dark and dangerous places. Every day, in small but definite ways, I turn from my baptismal identity as God's child, and construct a different identity, independent from him. At worst, I actively defy him, at 'best' I simply forget He is even there. Either way, I often fail to *live* as I fundamentally *am*: a beloved child of God. In short, I sin. However, despite all this – and this is the grace of my baptism – Christ has placed his indelible mark on my soul, and it is Christ himself who, when I stray, tugs at my heart and brings me home.

I am realising now that my entire spiritual life boils down to experiencing more fully, more deeply, that 'supernatural childhood' that He gave me at baptism. Inevitably, this demands a surrender of heart, an admission to the fact that I have a Perfect Father to whom I can entrust my whole life. It means turning away from a life without God and back towards the loving arms of a Father who is totally reliable and totally loving. Baptism was the start of my journey to holiness. All the other sacraments are there to help me complete it! At confession, I am restored to that baptismal innocence. Through the Eucharist, I am again brought into that baptismal unity with Christ, but this time in the form of bread and wine.

In my marriage, my soul is purified through a constant call to selfless love. I can easily be so unsure of my worth, and can find myself seeking the approval and honour of others. However, the Holy Spirit is a particularly good friend to me in this regard! I ask him, time and time again, to teach my heart more deeply of this knowledge of my true identity in Christ. At the start of each day, and in the face of any trial, I ask God's Holy Spirit to root me again in that foundational identity. It is the only foundation I have ever known to have never failed me!

Jared Harris, a recent graduate from Leeds Trinity University, passed through this initial sacramental threshold as an adult. His story speaks of the newness, liberation and belonging he felt when he was baptised:

I was baptised as an adult in 2014, whilst studying for a Theology degree at Leeds Trinity University. The sacrament had a great impact upon me then, and still has profound resonance for me today. What struck me most was the profession of faith and renouncing of evil, and the washing with water. During the profession of faith, I felt a great relief that what I had believed privately for a number of years could now finally be openly professed before the Church. My personal commitment to following God and rejecting evil was solemnly professed before the Church and my loved ones. It was not a new beginning in my faith journey, but my whole life in general. Through those baptismal waters, I truly felt I could let go of the sins and regrets of my past, and move forward. It is hard to explain the lightness I felt.

Although my problems didn't all disappear when I *was baptised* I felt that, with the Holy Spirit's help, I could now in a sense start again. I truly felt I had died with Christ to my old self and risen with him to a new life. It was real, and I had anticipated this moment for years. Being physically clothed with the white garment I felt, in a spiritual and material way, like I was beginning a new life. This personal conviction was confirmed when I proceeded, during the same Mass, to be confirmed and receive Jesus in Holy Communion. I also felt a deep bond with my Catholic friends as we could now receive the sacraments together; there was a great sense of community, which continues to this day.

In the weeks, months and years after that day I kept thinking back to what I had received, and it still has a deep impression on my soul. The trials of life did not disappear when I became a Christian, neither did my faults. In fact, there was a slight anti-climax when all the mundaneness of life carried on as usual as if nothing had changed. But deep down I know that something did change. On that day I became a child of God in a special way and through the help of his sacraments, I continue to become the person that God wills me to be.

Hannah Hayward (UK) is the Coordinating Lay Chaplain at Leeds Trinity University. She graduated from Leeds University in 2007 in Theology and International Development, BA, and worked as a Parish Youth Ministry Coordinator and Diocesan Youth Officer before taking up her current role. In 2012, she completed the Emmanuel School of Mission formation course in Rome.

Jesus Promised Power to His Believers
Fr Raniero Cantalamessa OFM Cap

Fr Raniero Cantalamessa OFM Cap, the preacher to the papal household for over 37 years, was professor of History of Ancient Christianity and the director of the Religious Sciences department at the University of Milan when he first came into contact with a new form of prayer, Charismatic Renewal, which changed his life and brought about a renewal of his baptism. Here is his story:

It was about 1975 that I first began to hear about a new way of praying. In the beginning, I was rather perplexed about it. So much so that I told a lady who asked my opinion about it not to attend any more of these prayer meetings. But eventually I decided to go and see what this was all about.

Frankly I was impressed. Studying the history of ancient Christianity, I could understand what was happening in these prayer meetings. For they were in fact very similar to what happened in the first Christian communities in the early Church. Yet it was something spontaneous and not done in imitation of them. I could see that it was a real thing, although going on in a new fashion. Some aspects, I must admit did strike me negatively, such as praying in tongues and some emotionalism I saw, but generally I was impressed.

133

The prayer groups asked me to give a few teachings, which I did, but I cannot say I was truly committed and held myself back. Then in 1977 a lady in Milan offered four tickets to go to the USA to attend the Kansas City conference, which was one of the first big ecumenical rallies among charismatics. I went and this turned out to be an important turning point for me.

It was quite an experience. There were 40,000 people there, 50 per cent Catholic and 50 per cent Protestant, all praying together. It was my first encounter with the face of the Charismatic Renewal. Parts of it attracted me very much but some aspects left me perplexed. After the conference was over an Irish priest invited the four of us to go to a retreat house in New Jersey. It was there that my conversion happened.

For me the big step was that of humility – to let a lay person pray over me, who already was a priest, a religious and a follower of St Francis – for the renewal of my baptism. In that moment I chose again Jesus as the Lord of my life. It was something very deep. As I lifted my eyes I saw the crucifix above the altar. I realised God was reminding me that this was the Jesus I was choosing as Lord and it was not an easy road. In this moment, I also realised that Charismatic Renewal is not something superficial or complementary but something that goes to the essential core of the Christian life – the power of the cross of Jesus.

The sign that something had happened at a deep level in my life, was the change in my prayer life. When I reached my friary in Washington, I found that I had such an attraction for prayer. This was a kind of honey-moon for me that continued for two months. It was the discovery of a new world that the majority of people don't know about. I feel the role of Charismatic Renewal is to open this door of experience and world of faith.

I was a happy religious in my vocation but the baptism in the Spirit has changed my life. Looking at my life I see it as the watershed of the two parts of my life. There was my life before the baptism in the Spirit and there has been my life after the baptism in the Spirit.

Why am I mentioning my experience? Because if we are to receive the Holy Spirit in this new, dramatic way, Scripture says that we must be baptised. But if we have already been baptised, there is need of a renewal of our baptism. For me, baptism in the Spirit was precisely this – a chance the Lord gave me to ratify and renew my baptism.

For most of us, baptism is a bound sacrament. That means that while we have received baptism in the Church, the Church gave it in the hope that at some point in our adult life we would confirm our 'I believe' in a personal, free act of faith. Until there is this act of faith in the life of a Christian, baptism remains a bound sacrament. Baptism allows us to receive Holy Communion but it also reveals why there are so many inactive Christians, passive and lacking any power. Jesus promised power to his believers, power enough to cast out demons and convict the world. Why, then are we so powerless?

Some months later in a moment of prayer I sensed a new call from the Lord – a very special call. It was as if Jesus was just in front of me, appearing in the same way that He did to the disciples when He came up from the Jordan and started preaching the Kingdom of God. I sensed an inner call and a voice which said, 'If you want to help me proclaim the Kingdom of God leave everything and follow me.' This meant, as I understood, 'Leave your teaching position and capacity as Director of the Religious Sciences department and come follow me.'

By the grace of God, by the end of the prayer I was able to surrender everything to the Lord and I had said 'Yes.' I went to see my superior general and asked to be allowed to leave my posts so I could follow this new vocation and go out and preach. He asked me to wait another year. And this is when obedience in the Church is so useful because it was like a confirmation, when the following year he recognised that this was a call from God and allowed me to leave the university in 1978. Three months later I was appointed to preach to the papal household.

Fr Raniero Cantalamessa OFM Cap (Italy) is a priest in the Order of Friars Minor Capuchin. He is a professor of Ancient Christianity, a scholar of Religion, international author and speaker. For 14 years, from 1994 to 2010 on the first channel of the Italian state television (RAI) he ran a weekly programme on the Gospel of the following Sunday. He has served as the preacher to the papal household since 1980 under St Pope John Paul II, Pope Emeritus Benedict XVI and Pope Francis.

For by one Spirit we were all baptised into one body – Jews or Greeks, slaves or free – and all were made to drink of one Spirit.

1 Corinthians 12:13

Through baptism each child is inserted into a gathering of friends who never abandon him in life or in death... This group of friends, this family of God, into which the child is now admitted, will always accompany him, even on days of suffering and in life's dark nights; it will give him consolation, comfort and light.

Pope Benedict XVI, 8 January 2006 (YouCat, Section Two)

Unless one is born of water and the Spirit, he cannot enter the Kingdom of God.

John 3:5

THE SACRAMENT OF MARRIAGE

The first natural tie of human society is man and wife.

St Augustine of Hippo

Love is patient and kind… Love does not insist on its own way… Love bears all things, believes all things, hopes all things, endures all things… Love never ends.

1 Corinthians 13:4-5, 7-8

'Authentic married love is caught up into divine love... so that this love may lead the spouses to God...' and in God they find the strength to carry on their roles and responsibilities.

Gaudium et Spes, 48

Sacrament of Matrimony[1]
Cardinal Luis Tagle

The Sacrament of Marriage or Matrimony is a covenant between a baptised man and woman. Together they form an intimate communion of life and love. This sacrament gives the husband and wife the grace to love each other with the love with which Christ has loved his Church. The apostle Paul, in his letter to the Ephesians reminds us, 'Husbands love your wives as Christ loved his Church' (Ephesians 5:25). This grace bestowed on them perfects the human love of the spouses, strengthens their indissoluble unity and sanctifies them on their way to eternal life.

Marriage, we may say, existed from the very beginning of time, it is as old as creation. We remember the creation of man and woman as partners sharing in the same human nature and dignity. They are meant to live together in a union of two loves. The passage in the book of Genesis reads:

And God blessed them, and God said to them, 'Be fruitful and multiply, and fill the earth and subdue it; and have dominion over the fish of the sea and over the birds of the air and over every living thing that moves upon the earth.'

---

1. This input is contributed by the Cardinal from his TV show *The Word Exposed*. For more teachings and inputs please visit: https://www.youtube.com/watch?v=VmZgKEp3K18 (last accessed 16 October 2017).

The *Catechism* teaches that

> Marriage is based on the consent of the contracting parties, that is, on their will to give themselves, each to the other, mutually and definitively, in order to live a covenant of faithful and fruitful love. (CCC 1662)

That is why the Catholic marriage requires four elements: first, the spouses are free to marry; second, they freely exchange their consent; third, in consenting to marry they have the intention to marry for life, to be faithful to one another, and be open to children; and fourth, their consent is given in the presence of two witnesses and before a properly authorised Church minister.

The mission of Adam and Eve to go forth and multiply is the same mission of all married couples. We are taught that marriage, by its very nature, is ordered to the good of the couple as well as to the generation and education of children. They are commissioned to build a Christian home, a place where children receive the first proclamation of the faith. Thus, the family, the home, is rightly called a domestic Church, a community of grace and prayer, a school of human virtues and of Christian charity.

Friends, most specially those who are married and those who are planning to get married, please keep in mind that marriage is a divine blessing that comes with great responsibility. You were chosen to be co-missionaries of God in His work of love. Keep the fire of your love for each other always burning, grow daily in faithful observance of the vows that you made at the altar, where Christ poured out His love for the Church. I know there will come a time when things get rough, but remember Jesus and His great love for the Church, that you now signify and represent – 'For better or for worse, for richer or for poorer, in sickness and in health.'

And when your love bears fruit in your children always look on them with love for they are the blessings of God to your marriage, to the Church, and to the World. Raise them as true Christians, following the footsteps of Christ, becoming good members of the Church and responsible citizens of society. And on that note, my dear friends, allow me to share how I am inspired and educated by the witness of loving and faithful couples. From my own parents I learned how patience and love conquer differences and faults. I learned how love is manifested in service to one another. I also learned from them that we are responsible for the wider family of the Church and society, thanks to my parents and the many wonderful parents in the world.

Cardinal Luis Tagle is Archbishop of Manilla and Cardinal of the Philippines. He is the President of Caritas International – a worldwide Catholic relief development and social service organisations – and the Catholic Biblical Federation. Cardinal Tagle became a Bishop in 2001 and was a former spiritual director and Rector in his own Diocesan seminary. He holds a doctorate in Sacred Theology.

Making Dreams Become Reality
Chris Padgett

A few months ago, Linda and I started a married couple's ministry called The Bar (Building Authentic Relationships). The premise is simple: we find a neutral location that will put people at ease, provide some alcohol and get to know the people who come. At the midpoint of the meeting we all sit and I ask a question for each couple to answer individually, and then share with their spouse. If they are open, they can share with the rest of the group what they discussed. It has been an exciting time for all involved.

Last night's question was predicated upon the fact that everyone would have celebrated Christmas before we met again, so I asked them to reflect upon your first Christmas together as a couple, or possibly your favourite gift from your spouse. One couple decided to share their memory, but as they began he said, 'I won't tell you what I got for my wife last year, because she didn't use it.' She looked at him and asked, 'What did you get me that I didn't use?' He said, 'A tombstone.' We all about fell out of our chairs laughing. Till death do us part is certainly stated in most couple's vows, but buying a tombstone may be pushing things a little.

In 1987, I met a girl in high school who willingly went out on a first date with me – an unknown and awkward goofball whose claim to fame was winning the senior superlative: Most

Unique Personality. We fell in love, and after a few years of dating we were married at the ripe old age of 21. This March, Linda and I will celebrate 25 years of marriage, and while it may be a cliché, I love her more today than I ever thought possible. So what tips can we offer on the Sacrament of Marriage?

There are three things I want to reflect upon when it comes to the importance of Catholic marriage. The first is the importance of growing together as a couple. The second addresses the necessity of being fully seen and learning to trust. And finally I will look at the joy of continuing to dream together.

As we begin, I first want to clarify a couple points. Catholicism says that marriage is a sacrament. There are necessary qualifications for this to be a sacramental marriage juxtaposed to a civil marriage, such as being free ecclesiastically, legally/ societally and personally to marry, and being baptised Catholics. With each couple willingly entering into the lifelong commitment of marriage, the union reflects Jesus' love for his Church. He is the bridegroom and we the Church are the bride. The intimacy and union in marriage, which bespeak God's love, is tangible in the sacramental union. Christ is present, in a true way within marriage, to enable the couples the ability to bring one another to Heaven. In other words, men have one job in marriage: to get their wife to Heaven. Women have one job as well, and while it may be more difficult, they also are called to get their husband to Heaven. The mutual self-giving provides an avenue of true sacramental grace to bring about this goal. The journey will take a lifetime, but this is as it should be. Nothing of value accidentally happens, including a joyful and successful marriage.

Marriage was never to be reduced down to simply passion between one another, nor is it about finding common interests, or even mutual attraction. Marriage is meant to reflect God's love in time, and this is not predicated upon one's passions, attractions or even mutual areas of interest. Marriage is a holy opportunity to witness to one another and the world what real love looks like, over a long period of time. Yes, this love will have passion, and hopefully attraction and common interests, but it is durable, even when we get old and saggy, find ourselves interested in a variety of other things our spouse isn't keen on, and strong even when our eyes dim as our older selves fade into our final years. With that in mind, let's quickly look at three tips for growing in one's marriage.

The first area worth exploring is the need for each couple to willingly grow together throughout the years. I am not necessarily talking about body sizes, although let's face it, we all seem to expand over time, and as I've joked, while our bodies are temples of the Holy Spirit, I've been feeding mine like it is a Basilica! I remember hearing from my parents that one of the reasons their marriage didn't last was that they grew and became interested in different things that took them

147

along different paths. This was always frustrating to me as a child, but even more so as an adult. Growing together, and finding peace in allowing one another to explore various new options, is something that is invaluable as a couple. You don't want to remain stagnant, so if one decides they want to try something new, I would advise doing this together. You will probably be stretched out of your comfort zone, but in the end it is worth being inconvenienced if it says to your spouse that you are willing for them to explore new avenues with them no matter what.

The second point is learning how to build a foundation of trust with your spouse. This happens when you quit pretending and trying to impress; rather, you allow your guard down and finally disclose who you are in all of its glory and mess. When a couple is together for a period of time, suddenly the truth of who each person is becomes quite clear. It is in the messy times that couples usually make a firm decision to either stick with one another or move on. In marriage, most couples have seen the good and the bad of their significant other. They accept these flaws and know God is at work. Over the years, couples recognise that while they still may be able to put on the charm at business meetings, or tell jokes that impress visiting friends, when everyone is gone and you are alone it isn't a joke or striking up the charisma that is needed in difficult moments. What is needed is authenticity. To love someone, even though they are broken and hurt, without excuse and yet still one you are committed to, I do believe that is where trust begins to thrive. In marriage, if you can have confidence that your spouse is with you in your place of authentic messiness, then you can breathe a sigh of relief knowing that a person is committed in our greatest and darkest hour. All marriages to really thrive need to be places of vulnerability and honesty.

Finally, the importance of a couple continuing to dream together cannot be overstated. I am amazed at how often couples seem to get lost in the regimented obligations and schedules of their daily tasks. Before they know it, the kids are out of school, out of the house and beginning their own lives. It is important for couples to continue to dream together, even during the busiest of times so that they build into one another's life hope of a future together, even when the little ones are grown and gone. Linda and I have practised this habit of dreaming together with diligence. I would even be so bold as to say it is one of the things we love most about being married. Every year we make a little sheet of paper for each of the kids to tell what dreams they want to go after for that year. As a family we help each other's dreams to become realities. We do the same for us as a couple. The other day, Linda and I went through our little dream journal and we marked dates for all of the things we had accomplished over the years. Seeing all of those dreams come true was so inspiring. We spent a lot of time dreaming big for our future. I wonder if you could be brave enough to try and imagine what seemingly impossible things you could try this year, not worrying about money and time, age or distance; just dreaming about what you want and working to make it happen. That is one of the greatest joys of marriage: helping one another's dreams come true!

In the end, when I think of all of the times we have spent together as a couple, I realise I am a better man because of her. She is working hard at getting me to Heaven, and I have a feeling she may need to be around for a lot longer to make that a reality. I am hoping that's the case because we have some amazing dreams to bring to fruition.

Chris Padgett (USA) is an international speaker and musician. Formerly of the Christian rock band Scarecrow and Tinman. Chris' ministries takes him around the world with concerts, keynotes, parishes as well as writing articles and interviews. Chris and his wife Linda Padgett live in Central New York, USA. You can read some of Linda's blogs at www. primalhappyplace.com and find out more about Chris and his ministry at www.chrispadgett.com.

Marriage
Editor with Charlotte Hibbert

My sister Katie is a stand-up comedian. A number of years back she was doing a gig and talking about her upcoming wedding. She was asking the audience what was the secret to a happy, lasting marriage? She asked who had been married the longest in the venue that night? One hand went up and said, 'Five years.' Another person said, 'Ten years' and then from the back of the room a man shouted, 'Twenty-nine years!' My sister looked at this man, and he looked like a real tough guy, a real bruiser, flat nose, large muscles with tattoos, wearing a vest. My sister remarked on the 29 years, that it seemed he had been married the longest out of everybody in the room, and she got him a round of applause. As the applause died down my sister asked him, 'So sir, if you have been married for twenty-nine years, what is the secret to a happy, lasting marriage?' He replied, 'Being in prison for twenty-eight years!'

So, what is the secret to a happy, lasting marriage?

Let's go back to where it all began: the Bible begins and ends with a marriage. So, if you weren't sure that God knows how to celebrate, He does! He even supplies the wine, that's Scripture (John 2:1-12). The Bible contains many references to marriage and there are images of marriages throughout Scripture, from

151

Adam and Eve all the way through to the Marriage Feast of the Lamb. A holy marriage is a sign of God himself and his overflowing love – for all creation (*YouCat*, 260). As St John Paul II reflected:

> The image of God is shown to us by the love between a man and woman, this in turn reflects the communion of love between the Father, the Son and Holy Spirit – the persons of the Trinity. (*Theology of the Body*, 9:3)

When a friend of mine was trying to find a wife, he was anxious about his quest. He was reassured by a priest who said, 'Don't worry someone out there has got your rib' (referencing Genesis 2:22-23). God's design is that holiness would enter the world through the union of man and woman. Together they are a visible sign to the world of the depths of God's love, which works powerfully within each of them and sustains their love for each other. We must realise too, that God loves us like that, but so much more!! The visible sign of marriage also reveals to the world Christ's love for the Church. Christ as the bridegroom and the Church as the bride. 'We are a living image of the love between Christ and the Church' (CCC 1664) (*YouCat*, 262). That is, Christ emptying himself out in love for his bride, the Church, and its members being invited to

> Love is perfected in fidelity.
> *Soren Kierkegaard*

empty themselves out in self-sacrificial love back to the bridegroom who is Christ. This love is so wondrous and so beautiful that it has to be a free choice, with no one being pressured or forced into it. As the Songs of Songs 2:16, says:

My beloved is mine and I am his.

A priest once asked a husband a hypothetical question, 'If you were in a boat with your wife and three children and the boat capsized, who would you rescue first?' The husband replied, 'The children of course.' The priest advised, 'You should swim to your wife first, if she tells you to rescue the children then do, but your first duty is to her.' Love and faithfulness within a marriage helps bring the husband and wife closer to Jesus; after all, their vocation is to get each other to heaven.

Why get married in a Church, why not just live together?

A marriage is between three people – the husband, the wife and God. God interjects the supernatural love and grace to flourish and sustain the marriage, that's why it's a sacrament. Let me put it this way, through the sacrament, a couple invite God into their union and closeness with one another and through that unity God has the opportunity to purify and make beautiful the relationship. True love does not come from ourselves, but is poured into us from God who is love

(Romans 5:5), since wherever there is love there is God (1 John 4:8). Therefore, with God's help and love, the married couple are given the grace and strength to endure. Marriage in Christ signifies their faithfulness to one another because where there is no loyalty to the other person there cannot be true love.

Moving in with someone is a short-term commitment; it does not involve the same lifetime sacrifice that marriage requires. If you want to focus on finding your other half's weaknesses, sins and failures, you will find them. But faithfulness is what God is about, and what He teaches us. We see that throughout the course of history. God is faithful to his people, to those He enters into a relationship with, He never fails them. People can be unfaithful to their promises but He, as the third person in the marriage is never unfaithful. Through the grace of the sacrament, He is able to change each person so that they 'rely upon God's help rather than one's own resources of love', as with Christ a couple can kindle hope against hope (*YouCat*, 263, 269). God is not fully part of your

Christ chose to be born and grow up in the bosom of the holy family of Joseph and Mary. The Church is nothing other than 'the family of God'. From the beginning, the core of the Church was often constituted by those who had become believers 'together with all [their] household'. When they were converted, they desired that 'their whole household' should also be saved. These families who became believers were islands of Christian life in an unbelieving world.

CCC 1655

relationship, your home or your family unless He is present through the Sacrament of Marriage.

There's a guy I know who went overseas to invest in a promising business venture. Unfortunately, he suffered calamity after calamity; for one reason or another, he found he had lost most of his money. He knew he had to make the most difficult phone call of his life, to ring his wife back home and let her know. He was in tears over the phone as he explained he had lost everything and he was so sorry. His wife told him to just come home as it wasn't the money she wanted, it was him.

In our society, marriage is tested like no other institution, but this should be seen as a challenge to refine a husband and wife and increase their faithfulness to one another. That faithfulness comes from a sense that they have been called to this special vocation from God himself and that it is one of his greatest gifts to humanity. St Pope John Paul II in his extensive writings on the beauty and wonder of marriage reflected on all this, as he taught that as Christ gives of himself self-sacrificially to the Church, the Church is invited to give of themselves totally: so a husband should give of himself self-sacrificially as the wife does totally. But he added in love, that's why contraception is a lie because it says to the other I love you and I give of myself, totally, unconditionally,

> Even as you seek a virtuous, fair, and good spouse... it is fitting that you should be the same.
>
> *St Bernardino of Siena*

to you but I hold back part of myself from you, my fertility. There should be no barriers to this unconditional love. This is why Natural Family Planning has become a great gift within the Church, helping couples plan their lives and families.

Why is the Church against sex outside of marriage?

The Church is against the marital act outside of marriage because only within a marriage are you fully able to give yourself to another. When a married couple are intimate, they gift themselves to the other: their past, present and their future. However, pre-marital relationships are not fully committed relationships, as there is always an exit option. A priest friend gave a talk about the theology of the body to a class of teenagers. At the end of the talk a teenage girl asked, 'Father, when do you know if you are ready?' The priest replied, 'Look at the second finger on your left hand, is there a ring on it?' She said, 'No.' He stated: 'Then you are not ready.'

> Husbands, love your wives, as Christ loved the Church and gave himself up for her, that he might sanctify her, having cleansed her by the washing of water with the word... Even so husbands should love their wives as their own bodies.
>
> *Ephesians 5:25-26, 28*

God is not against sex, He created it, but it is so high a gift, so beautiful a wonder, that He does not want it used in the wrong context. It is referred to as the 'marital act' as that is what it is. A wife and husband exchange vows at the altar, but their marriage is not consummated until they come together in the marital act. The act is so full of beauty and wonder once you are married, as God has entered your relationship from the altar, as Jesus taught so beautifully during his public ministry what marriage and this holy union in God is (Matthew 19:4-7).

Pre-marital relationships can harm the dignity of a person. I have a friend who as a teenager started going out with someone, he put pressure on her to sleep with him. She didn't want to, but she thought that if she didn't then she may lose him, so she gave in. A few months later he left her and she said it was like a part of her heart had been ripped out. The marital act isn't just a physical closeness; it involves the heart and soul. My friend then went out with another guy and exactly the same thing happened. After a short time, he left her and she said again it was like having a part of her heart ripped out. This situation reoccurred so often, that in the end, she said it was like having a plaster taken off her heart and put back on again. She was broken and in bits, but she found God's mercy and love through confession, found redemption and went on to be happily married with a beautiful family.

Intimacy without commitment and God's grace is dangerous and can break hearts as we create spiritual bonds with others.

What is God's role in a marriage?

In marriage, couples are called to live out their first vocation to holiness by being Christ to each other. But how are they supposed to be Christ to each other when distracted by daily frustrations? Being able to accept each other's flaws and weaknesses and learning to grow in forgiveness is a fundamental part of marriage. As Colossians teaches, the best safeguard against sin is love and as the book of Proverbs, 17:9, says: 'He who forgives an offence seeks love.'

Marriage is difficult, everybody is human and nobody is perfect. That is why there is a need for a third person in the marriage and to go back to him, as God, is the source of strength that you need on those difficult days. God will always signpost back to your spouse and vice versa. St Teresa of Kolkata would get people coming to her convent wanting to volunteer and asking what they could do, she would ask them if they were married. If she found out they were, she would tell them to go back to their homes to love and serve their families. People can get caught up with wanting to do great works of mercy and mission outside of their homes, out in the world, which is great and so needed, but married people must not forget their first mission is to serve their spouse. As Mother Teresa would say, 'See in your spouse, sometimes in their weakness in their faults, in their sin the distressing disguise of Christ.'

> Better to instruct a child than to collect riches.
>
> *St Herve of Brittany*

Love always takes the form of service, as we love our spouse, we love Christ. That's the sacrament. St Teresa says for married couples this is their primary calling, their vocation. There can be so many distractions that draw couples away from married life such as work, lust, pornography, and so on. This is why it is so important to have God as the centre of any marriage.

Where can division and deception in a marriage come from?

If God's purpose is to unite us, the devil's purpose is to divide us. It is sin that leads a couple to point out each other's faults; through love they are able to forgive the failings and draw one another together in spite of weaknesses. As we see from the example of Adam and Eve, the devil divided and deceived so he could accuse. Through this division, the devil tried to dismantle the union Adam and Eve had in God. Similarly today, a spouse should not take on the role of an accuser, because that will divide and separate. Instead, they should work with each other's faults and weaknesses. Marriages fail when couples cannot forgive each other's imperfections. God teaches us that nobody is perfect or sinless and that couples must, through God's grace, continuously forgive one another and protect each other against accusations and division. They are each other's armour and a spouse's role is to protect the other from sin, which separates and destroys divine life within each one of us. There

> Guided and strengthened by God's grace husband and wife 'advance their own perfection, as well as their mutual sanctification, and hence contribute jointly to the glory of God.'
>
> *Gaudium et Spes, 48*

is a true story of St Thérèse of Lisieux, who had a vision one day; in the vision Jesus brought her into a room full of crosses and invited her to pick one. She picked the largest cross in the room; Jesus said she could not have it. When she asked why, He said, 'Because it's reserved for married couples.'

What does the Church mean when it talks about a domestic Church?

A domestic Church is the family, who create a miniature Church within their home. If it is God's design, each couple is called to be open to children, so their family is called to be a domestic Church where love and joy are nurtured. A domestic Church is a smaller iteration of your parish Church, made present within your own homes and families. As the Trinity are a community of persons, so the family are an image of God's love in human fellowship. They become a light to the world. The family, through God's love, can reveal to the world the joy, peace, laughter and love of the Trinity.

The celebration of a marriage is an important and joyous occasion for families and communities. The wedding itself is an opportunity to share the joy the husband and wife have for each other. The Sacrament of Marriage and the celebration of family is pre-empting the Marriage Feast of the Lamb, when in all eternity we will be so intimately united to God with a joy and peace beyond all comprehension, way past any or all our expectations (1 Corinthians 2:9).

What Do 'Soulmates' and Santa Clause Have in Common?

Jason Evert

When my parents broke the news to me that Santa Claus didn't exist, I stormed out of the room, blurting, 'I don't even want to know about the Easter Bunny!' Although the news was devastating at the time, I found solace in the fact I had obtained a more realistic grasp of how gifts arrived under our tree. Letting go of a childish notion of St Nick also paved the way for me to obtain a mature understanding of St Nicholas, the saintly bishop of the fourth century.

What does all of this have to do with finding 'the one'? Well, many people have a notion of soulmates that's in need of serious demythologising. In exchange, they can discover a mature Christian concept of their future (or current) spouse.

In his ancient text, *The Symposium*, Plato presents the myth that men and women originally had four arms, four legs, and two faces. Unfortunately, Zeus split them in half as a punishment for their pride (which conveniently doubled his number of worshippers). Meanwhile, these incomplete individuals wandered the earth until they found their other halves. Upon discovering the other, the two would know they were made for one another, and would finally become whole.

Plato explains:

After the division the two parts of man, each desiring his other half, came together, and throwing their arms about one another, entwined in mutual embraces, longing to grow into one, they were on the point of dying from hunger and self-neglect, because they did not like to do anything apart. (*The Symposium*)

Sounds more like Hollywood than Plato.

Looking for your better half?

We should not expect another person to complete us. Let God do that. Some guys think, 'Since a wife is supposed to be your better half, I guess I'm only fifty per cent complete until I find her. When I find her, she will fill my emptiness and take care of all of my emotional needs.' If this guy finds a girl, it will not be a budding relationship; it will be a hostage situation.

Nevertheless, Hollywood has made a fortune perpetuating the eternal myth that there is a perfect person out there for each of us. But here's the problem: You're going to have to wait a lifetime before you can marry a perfect person. (For those familiar with the book of Revelation, I'm referring to the Wedding Feast of the Lamb.) Until then, anyone you marry is going to have his or her share of imperfections.

Sorry to be the bearer of bad news, but in this life, you're not going to find someone with whom you are perfectly compatible. After all, the word 'compatible' comes from the

Latin *compati*, which means to 'suffer with' (*com* 'with', *pati* 'to suffer'). Successful marriages are not the result of finding a perfect person, but rather loving the imperfect person who you have chosen to marry. St Francis de Sales even described marriage as 'a perpetual exercise of mortification.'

Only God can complete us. When we make an idol out of a relationship, we are setting ourselves up for disappointment because all idols are meant to be broken.

Do soulmates exist?

If there's no perfect person made only for you, should we conclude from this that there's no heavenly plan for your love life? In a blog in which he makes many excellent points, Matt Walsh wrote, 'My wife and I weren't destined for each other. It wasn't fate that brought us together. We are bound not by karma, but by our choice.'[1] He goes on to say that God doesn't destine us to end up with anyone specific. Rather, there are countless people whom we could marry and be equally content. They become our soulmates when we marry them. We don't marry them because they are our soulmates.

While there is some merit to these ideas, the difficulty with this concept is that it doesn't leave much room for divine providence. For those theologians out there, it sounds more

---

1. http://www.theblaze.com/contributions/i-didnt-marry-the-one-she-become-the-one-after-i-married-her (last accessed 16 October 2017).

deist than theist. (Deism being the view that God exists, but that He is not directly involved in the world.)

In the book of Tobit, the archangel Raphael declares to Tobias, regarding his future wife, 'Do not be afraid, for *she was destined for you from eternity...* When Tobias heard these things, he fell in love with her and yearned deeply for her' (Tobit 6:17).

This isn't Hollywood; it's the Sacred Scriptures. We know Adam was made for Eve, Sarah was destined for Tobias, Joseph was created for Mary, and so on. But how, when, and why does God choose to play the role of a heavenly matchmaker?

Obviously, only God knows the answer to this. But we know that divine providence intervenes in our lives to the extent that we make room for it. Those who walk with God often marvel at how He seems to intervene in the most providential ways in the tiniest details of life. Believers routinely speak of 'divine appointments', and other occasions where we can see God's hand at work.

For example, Mother Teresa (St Teresa of Calcutta [Kolkata]) once said that a man came to her, seeking a specific medicine for his dying child. However, the drug could not be obtained in India. As she was speaking to the man, someone walked into the convent with a basket of half-used medicines. Right on top of the basket was the rare drug. She remarked:

I just couldn't believe because if it was inside, I would not have seen it. If he had come before or after, I would not have connected. I just stood in front of that basket and kept looking at the bottle and in my mind I was saying, 'Millions and millions and millions of children in the world how could God be concerned with that little child in the slums of Calcutta. To send that medicine, to send that man just at that time, to put that medicine right on the top and to send the full amount that the doctor had prescribed.' See how precious that little one was to God himself. How concerned He was for that little one.

If God is infinitely concerned with providing medicine to his children, you can rest assured He is also interested in providing for our vocations. I believe God the Father has a perfect plan for each of our lives, just as He had for his own Son. However, as Isaiah 55:9 tells us, 'For as the heavens are higher than the earth, so are my ways higher than your ways and my thoughts than your thoughts.' Sometimes this 'perfect' plan involves substantial suffering, but this does not make it any less perfect. Its perfection comes from the fact that it comes from the heart of a Father who loves us.

What this means is that God doesn't promise that you'll find the person who makes you the happiest, but if you remain open to his will, you'll discover the person who will make you the Holiest – and this will bring you more joy in the end than any plan you could have concocted without him. Your *soul* will be sanctified through this *mate*... and in my opinion, that's God's idea of blessing you with a soulmate.

Jason Evert (USA) is an international author and Chasity speaker who has founded Totus Tuus Press and the chastityproject.com. He has spoken on six continents about the virtue of chastity. He is the author of more than ten books, including *How to Find Your Soulmate without Losing Your Soul* and *Theology of the Body for Teens*. This reflection from him and other reflections from him and the chastity project team can be found at: http://chastityproject.com/2015/03/ soulmates-santa-claus-common/(last accessed September 2017).

4 Secrets to Sexual Healing

Crystalina Evert

I've always said that it's possible to start over, regardless of the past. But what does that mean? It's one thing to decide to start over, but it's another thing to figure out what to do with the effects of the past.

You don't just hear a riveting chastity talk and sign a fresh purity commitment card, and then everything is restored. What's often unseen is the drawn-out process of untying the knots.

As many of you know, I was raised in a broken family, lost my virginity at the age of fifteen, and lived through abusive and unfaithful relationships. Some of my wounds were self-inflicted because of my own poor choices, while others were inflicted upon me.

Before meeting my husband, I quit living my crazy lifestyle and began to practise purity. But what about the wounds of the past? I stuffed them. We women are masters at stuffing our stuff. We put our makeup on, buy a new wardrobe, and offer the world a big fake smile. But inside, we're afraid to start crying because we're afraid we'll never stop. So, we numb ourselves with false consolations.

How do we (both men and women) stop running from the past and learn how to face it, own it, and heal it? Here are my four keys:

167

Go to counselling

Most people feel embarrassed to seek professional help. We want everyone (especially ourselves) to think we have it all together. But we'll never solve a problem until we admit that it exists. Because I spent years of my life running from the past, my life became an intricate web of coping mechanisms. I began to identify with my brokenness, thinking that my tough exterior façade was my identity. Actually, it wasn't me at all. It was the frightened girl who wanted to keep everyone at bay because she knew that vulnerability leads to pain. But this isn't any way to live. It's just existing. This isn't how to thrive or glorify God. So, get over your fears and talk to someone who can help you to finally slay them. Go to womenmadenew.com or catholictherapists.com to find a counsellor.[1]

Go to the Eucharist

I knew that in my healing process, I could only go so far by myself. After many of my counselling sessions, I needed to process my thoughts and emotions. So, I ran to God in Eucharistic Adoration. I would pray, journal, and even cry in his Holy Presence. It was there in those quiet chapels that God was able to begin mending so many of my open wounds.

---

1. Though these websites do not detail UK therapists, the website catholictherapists.com has counsellors who can counsel via Skype and it may be possible that they can put people in touch with UK counsellors.

With him by my side, I felt safe going into the dark places of my memories. It was scary at times to face them, but I learned that only Jesus could undo some of the things that had been done.

Find a good priest

Going to a counsellor is essential if you've suffered serious emotional wounds. But a good priest is invaluable in the healing process as well because it can be tough to decipher what issues are emotional and which are spiritual. After all, human efforts alone can only accomplish so much. Because we have souls, we often need deliverance and divine intervention. We can't expect the couch of a counsellor to erase what needs to be healed in the confessional, and vice versa.

Find fellowship

When you're drumming up all the wounds of the past, the devil will try to rub your nose in them. He wants you to think that you're just an unlovable, helpless mess. At times like this, it's essential to have family, friends, or some other support system that will accept you where you're at, reminding you that you are lovable, even if you are a mess! Therefore, don't try to heal alone.

If you don't know a good friend, priest, or counsellor who would stand by your side, pray that God would show you where to find them, so that they can help you to carry your cross.

It doesn't matter who you are or what has happened to you. All that matters now is where you go from here. As I once heard, 'No matter how dirty your past is, your future is still spotless.'

Crystalina Evert (USA) has spoken internationally to hundreds of thousands of people with her message of the beauty of chastity and God's plan for human sexuality. She is the founder of Women Made New Ministries – which encourages women in need of personal healing, helping them to be the women God created them to be. She is also co-founder of the Chastity Project – where this reflection and other resources are available. She is an international author of books, including *Pure Womanhood.* The article above can also be found at https://chastityproject.com/2014/10/four-secrets-sexual-healing/ (last accessed September 2017).

Marriage, a Unique Sacrament

Marianne and Matthew Barnes

Marriage is a unique sacrament. It is the only sacrament that is shared between two people. Two people committing themselves with words spoken before God, words that echo through heaven, binding them for the rest of their lives on earth.

When I think about the moment I realised Matthew was 'the one' I find it difficult to pinpoint the exact time and place; rather, it was after a series of discussions I'd had with a holy woman and a holy man, a Carmelite nun behind bars (not prison bars obviously) and a priest during confession. It wasn't a lightning-bolt moment, it wasn't even anything Matthew did particularly that made me think 'Yep that man's for keeps.' It was after a series of open and honest heartfelt conversations with these particularly wise people that brought me to the knowledge that he was indeed my soulmate.

In my teenage years, I remember praying after receiving communion, 'Please Lord I'd rather be single for ever than have a rubbish man in my life' and I genuinely meant it. Maybe it was being the youngest of five and all my elder siblings having partners or husbands/wives at the time, but the concept of bringing a young man home to meet my family filled me with utter dread. I was the baby, they would undoubtedly poke fun at me and wind me up something rotten, so at the time I met Matthew this was not something I was looking forward to.

Matthew, on the other hand, could not wait to get into a relationship. He tried to use prayer as a divine love potion, 'Please Lord make her fancy me, please Lord I want to marry *her*, also can I have a Ferrari and a castle.' Thankfully God laughed at his plans and Matthew soon realised it was better to accept God's plan for him and started believing in divine providence. He found that it was better to ask God to help him realise what was best for him, rather than using prayer as a wish list. He started to pray for help in overcoming obstacles that were preventing him being the best version of himself. More importantly, he began asking God to reveal his plan, whether it involved marriage, the single life, priesthood or religious.

We met each other in Lourdes, travelling as youth helpers, I was 17 and he was 18. He caught my attention at the dinner table in the hotel we were all staying, not because of his dashing good looks and smart get-up. No, in fact, he had shoulder-length greasy hair and an old bobbly fleece on. It was the way he held the attention of every person around him and how they were all hysterically laughing. I thought to myself 'Oh he looks like a laugh, I'll go and see what all the fun is about', only to find as soon as I sat down near him he blushed and went completely quiet.

We struck up an instant friendship and remained friends for a year, meeting at the planned reunions and nights out. The year after, we both went to World Youth Day in Cologne, Germany. This was a two-week trip which would start in Schoenstatt and end with Mass by Pope Benedict XVI in a field with over a million other young people. We drank German beer, sang Bavarian songs, danced on tables and talked and laughed, we really got to know each other and the spark was lit.

Our relationship developed further a few years later after we attended a reconciliation service at Our Lady's Shrine in Walsingham. The priest had asked me if I was considering marriage, he said that if I was serious about this relationship, it was important that we got to know each other spiritually and emotionally before getting to know each other physically. This gave me food for thought and when I shared this with Matthew, he told me that he was encouraged to write a prayer as his penance; so together we wrote a prayer, sat in a hayfield in Walsingham, and have continued to say it every day since. Even when we are apart this prayer brings us together:

Dear Lord,

Thank you for bringing us together,

Thank you for all the blessings you have bestowed upon us, individually and as a couple,

We ask for your continued help and guidance, that we may have a strong relationship now and forever,

Help us to grow together, spiritually, emotionally, physically
    and psychologically
Help us to love each other, but above all help us to love,
    together, our faith, our church and you our blessed father.
Amen.

We dated for around five years before we got engaged and were married the year after.

Faith and spirituality has always been a big part of our relationship. We have always tried to encourage one another to deepen our knowledge and encounter Christ's spirit here on earth. We are blessed that we have had positive experiences and role models that have encouraged us to have a faith. We have always tried to get involved with the Church where possible, whether this was volunteering our time for youth programmes or now just being part of the parish community. The purpose of marriage for me is building one another up so that you can be the best versions of yourself, who God wanted you to be.

We have both grown in confidence in our marriage, always knowing that we have the unwavering support and love of our partner. My prayer is that we will always love each other and continue to grow together in our marriage, and with God's help I know that we will.

Matthew and Marianne Barnes reside in the Diocese of Salford. They have been married six years and currently have two young sons. They are actively involved in their parish and wider community, in particular, leading marriage preparation and marriage enrichment courses and are members of the Diocesan Marriage and Family Life Committee, helping to bring the teachings of Pope Francis' encyclical *Amoris Laetitia* to all parishes within their Diocese.

Have you not read that he who made them from the beginning made them male and female... For this reason a man shall leave his father and mother and be joined to his wife, and the two shall become one. So they are no longer two but one. What therefore God has joined together, let no man put asunder.

Matthew 19:5-6

No one is without a family in this world: the Church is a home and family for everyone especially those who 'labour and are heavy laden.'

St Pope John Paul II

The family is, so to speak, the domestic Church. In it parents should, by their word and example be the first preachers of the faith to their children.

Lumen Gentium, 11

THE SACRAMENT OF HOLY ORDERS
(PRIESTHOOD)

Priesthood is the love of the heart of Jesus. When you see a priest, think of our Lord Jesus Christ.

St John Vianney

Like living stones be yourselves built into a spiritual house, to be a holy priesthood, to offer spiritual sacrifices acceptable to God through Jesus Christ.

1 Peter 2:5

The priest continues [Christ's] work of redemption on earth.

St John Vianney

Discovering the 'More'

Christina Lynas

It was the 5 April 2007, Holy Thursday. I sat in a small chapel in an old country house in the middle of the highlands of Scotland and it was the last place I wanted to be. My eldest sister had managed to talk me into going on retreat with her for the Easter Triduum and now I found myself with all these happy-clappy Christians who wanted to hug me. What had I got myself into?! Their joy and happiness annoyed me but I couldn't work out why... I believed in Jesus and went to church on Sundays but couldn't exactly call myself a good Catholic. I struggled with a lot of the teachings of the Church and had decided to live my faith on my own terms. For me the most important thing was to be nice and kind, so as long as I wasn't hurting other people then what was so wrong with the way I was living my life?

'Guilt, good old Catholic guilt. I am sure most of us knows what that feels like.' The voice of the priest penetrated my daydream. Guilt. Yes, I knew all about that! I broke the rules, I felt guilty, I went to confession, I still felt guilty, I broke the rules again. This was the vicious circle of my life!

'This is NOT why Jesus came! This is NOT what Jesus wants for us!' Hmmm, the priest had my attention now...

'Jesus died, Jesus was tortured and freely embraced his cross, to wipe away all guilt! This is WHY Jesus came. Not

179

to trap you in a life of guilt but to bring you to new life, a life of fullness, a life of TRUE freedom!'

I have no idea what else the priest or anyone else said to me the rest of that day, but these words had struck a chord with me and started whirring around in my head... So, is there another way?

The next morning – Good Friday – we were to climb a hill and pray the Stations of the Cross as we climbed. Before we climbed, one of the leaders said to me very gently and quietly, almost as if they were sharing a treasured secret with me, 'You know, if you had been the only one alive, Jesus still would have endured all his passion, just to save you. That is how much He loves you!' And off we went climbing up this steep hill with readings of his torture and pain echoing through my ears. 'Really Lord?' my heart questioned. 'Do you really care about my life, about my sins? Was this for me?'

The answer to these questions came just hours later. We all gathered to watch *The Passion of Christ*, a film I had never seen before but had heard the stories of how realistic it was. As I watched the love of Christ portrayed in each scene I was struck to the core, my heart moved with compassion and sorrow for all He endured. Then there was a moment, just as Jesus was carrying his cross, when He fell and looked directly at the screen. In this moment it was as if Christ was looking straight into my eyes, into my heart, and with such sorrow He whispered, 'This one was for you.' In an instant I knew that my sins *were* hurting someone. They were hurting Christ himself. Tears rolled down my cheeks and I wept through the end of the film. I now knew how desperately I needed to confess. Confessions were being heard in the next room and I rushed to join the short line.

As I walked in I was greeted with a warm and welcoming smile and then I began to confess. In my confession, I mentioned that I had said some of these sins before.

'Do you believe God has forgiven you?' the priest asked.

'I don't know,' was my reply.

'Do you believe He can?'

Again: 'I don't know.'

The priest challenged me with light and caring humour, 'Who are you, to say to God, "There's this one sin you can't or won't forgive."'

'Well, when you look at it like that...' I smiled.

'God has forgiven you all your sins, go in peace.' As I left, I *knew*, perhaps for the first time, that I was forgiven!

As my penance, I had to go into the chapel and lay my guilt down on the altar and leave it there, free of it. As I sat in this quiet chapel, I felt a deep sense of peace and then in the silence I felt the Lord speak to my heart: 'I want so much *more* for you than this.'

I knew these words to be a plea for me to change the way I was living, a plea from someone who loved me more than I could imagine, and I knew I had to try.

181

Ten years on I thank God for the profound grace of that confession, the truth that the priest spoke to me and the complete transformation that has taken place in my life. After that weekend I searched to know the Lord and our Church and to wrestle with all its teachings. The more I studied the more I discovered the love and beauty that lies behind each one of these teachings. I have discovered the **more** that God wanted for me. This **more** is my living relationship with him, meeting with him in the sacraments, living in freedom of guilt and of fear, trusting in his great love for me and trusting in who He is; God Almighty, Creator of Heaven and Earth, my Father, my friend.

Thank you Lord for your love, your mercy and you priests!

The following passage is a constant reminder of the Father's love for me: Matthew 6:24-34:

No one can serve two masters; for a slave will either hate the one and love the other, or be devoted to the one and despise the other. You cannot serve God and wealth. Therefore I tell you, do not worry about your life, what you will eat or what you will drink, or about your body, what you will wear. Is not life more than food, and the body more than clothing? Look at the birds of the air; they neither sow nor reap nor gather into barns, and yet your heavenly Father feeds them. Are you not of more value than they? And can any of you by worrying add a single hour to your span of life? And why do you worry about clothing? Consider the lilies of the field, how they grow; they neither toil nor spin, yet I tell you, even Solomon in all his glory was not clothed like one of these. But if God so clothes the grass of the field, which is alive today and tomorrow is thrown into the oven, will he not much more clothe you – you of little faith? Therefore do not worry, saying, 'What will we eat?' or 'What will we drink?' or 'What will we wear?' For it is the Gentiles who strive for all these things; and indeed your heavenly Father knows that you need all these things. But strive first for the kingdom of God and his righteousness, and all these things will be given to you as well. So do not worry about tomorrow, for tomorrow will bring worries of its own. Today's trouble is enough for today.

Christina Lynas (UK) is the former managing director of Youth 2000, UK, who specialises in Youth Ministry and Mission; and who was also a former member of the Craig Lodge Community, a retreat centre in Dalmally, Scotland.

One Miracle Every Day

Fr Lee Marshall

On a recent pilgrimage to Lourdes, a 15-year-old boy approached me after a Holy Hour of Adoration of the Blessed Sacrament – which it had been my privilege to lead. 'Father,' he said in a serious tone, 'I need to speak to you. Something happened to me during the Holy Hour!' I listened with wonder as he continued: 'As you exposed the Blessed Sacrament, I felt a heavy pressure pushing against my heart. Then I heard Jesus speak to me. The Lord asked me to follow him. In a vision I saw myself following Jesus… He turned towards me, showing his hands, and revealed that He desired me to become a priest.' At this point my young friend said he felt tears in his eyes. The strange force continued to press against his heart for the whole hour of prayer. Once the Blessed Sacrament was reposed, the pressure mysteriously lifted.

Encounters like this are not uncommon. The following day a young lady aged 16 approached me. She was beaming with joy. During that same Holy Hour she revealed that she had wept throughout, and described how through her tears, the pain she had felt inside for so long poured out of her. She had been full of joy ever since.

Strictly speaking, we might not define these two encounters as miraculous, but they are just two examples of the signs and wonders I have experienced week in, week out in my few short years as a priest. Catholics believe that Jesus is truly present in the Blessed Sacrament; He is no less present in the Mass than I am present – my body with its living blood flowing through my veins and of course the precious gift I carry, my soul. The Body of Christ, his Precious Blood and his Soul are also present in the Eucharist. This is truly awesome, but there's more, much more. His Divinity is also present: this means that Almighty God is present in the Eucharist! Is it any wonder that young men hear his call when they open their hearts and adore him? Is it any wonder that young women receive powerful inner healings in his presence? Of course not: the only wonder is that more people don't experience his presence in the Eucharist.

As a priest, I witness at least one miracle every day, at the moment I raise the bread and wine with my hands and they are no longer bread and wine, but the Body and Blood of Jesus Christ. One of the greatest joys of the priesthood occurs when the Lord reveals his miraculous presence in the Eucharist to those who it is my great privilege to serve.

After my young friend in Lourdes had finished recounting his testimony, I enquired, 'So how do you feel about becoming a priest?' He thought for a moment, then shrugged his shoulders, looked at me and said: 'It's not such a bad idea!'

Fr Lee Marshall (UK) is a priest for the Diocese of Hallam currently serving as Catholic Chaplain to Sheffield and

Sheffield Hallam Universities. A regular homilist/speaker for Youth 2000 UK, he was formerly a financial director of a large architect firm.

Priesthood

Editor with Fr Julian Green

In 2001, I felt God was calling me to the priesthood, so I applied. During this period, I said a prayer to Our Lady: 'If this is what your Son wants for me, send me a sign – a statue of yourself.' I thought that was a fair deal; I give my life to her Son and all she has to do is to produce one single statue. At the end of the year-long application process, I was not accepted. I went back to my career in show business.

Four years later I felt the call again, but this time door after door seemed to be opening for me to start my formation at seminary. I had forgotten that initial prayer all those years ago, but while attending a Catholic Conference, a lady I knew from Liverpool walked up to me and, pointing to a statue of Our Lady on the

> The government of souls is the art of arts.
>
> *St Gregory the Great*

altar, asked me if I liked it. 'Yes, I love it, it's beautiful,' I replied. 'That's my own personal statue. I lent it to the Conference for the weekend. People ask me if they can have it but I always say no.' Then she looked at me and said, 'Would you like it?' She didn't have to ask twice!

A short time later when visiting my spiritual director, he said, 'Before we start today I want to show you something.' He brought me into a small room where there was a statue of Our Lady. Then he said, 'This was donated to the chaplaincy but I really feel you should have it.' Are you keeping count?! On the day of my Ordination the Irish singer, Dana, and her husband, Damien, who are great friends of my family, presented me with a gift. It was a rectangular box, I shook it lightly, thought to myself could it really be? I took off the wrapping paper slowly, opened the lid of the box and guess what was inside the box? A statue – of St Anthony of Padua! I'm kidding. It was of Our Lady. That summer when I was on pilgrimage in Lourdes, I was sharing with a friend about the experience of receiving the first statue, then the second statue and then that third experience and she said, 'Well, that's Our Lady for you.' I said, 'What?' She said, 'That's Our Lady for you.' I said, 'What do you mean?' She said, 'Well, she's not once, not twice, but three times a Lady!'

> Thou art a priest for ever, after the order of Melchizedek.
>
> *Hebrews 7:17*

Just as our earthly lives are formed in the wombs of our mothers and nurtured under their care, so are priestly vocations formed and nurtured under Our Lady's care. When people see a statue of Our Lady they immediately think of Catholicism (even though she is the heavenly mother of all disciples). Sadly, when people want to attack the Catholic Church, it is often a statue of Our Lady they desecrate. This happened in the church in Mosul when terrorists brutally tore down a statue of Our Lady (which was later prayerfully reinstated when Iraqi soldiers from the Babylonian brigade rescued the city). Our Lady is recognised as Mother by all Catholics: Mother of the Church and Mother of us all. But for the priest, Mary is Mother in a particular way, for he sacramentally embodies her Son Jesus Christ, so he is related to the Mother of Christ in a more intimate way. In fact, the saints refer to the priest as 'another Christ'.

> Every baptised person is a member of the Priestly People of God and therefore represents Christ; and just as Jesus offered his life up to the Father on the cross, so we are all called to offer up our own lives to the Father. This is what is known as the 'common priesthood'. When a priest is ordained he does not stop being a member of this Priestly People of God, but his relationship to Jesus is intensified and acquires a new aspect. (*Lumen Gentium*, 11)

The priesthood – a new dimension

Jesus Christ is the one Mediator between God and men (1 Timothy 2:5). What is a mediator? When there is a dispute between two people, a mediator is the person who steps in between the two to try to draw them closer. Jesus Christ, however, is a greater Mediator than someone who just steps in between God and people to resolve the crisis of sin. Our faith proclaims that Jesus Christ is both true God and true man: He doesn't just step in-between, He himself is the reconciliation between God and humankind. Jesus' role as Mediator is seen most visibly when He hung upon the cross between heaven and earth. With his arms open He embraces the world, his head towards heaven and his feet towards earth drawing all people to himself in order to bring them to his Father (John 12:32). He doesn't just offer himself to the Father, He brings all of us – with all of our sins, weaknesses, brokenness and vulnerability – through his own body into friendship with God.

That is what a priest does! His role is to draw people into deeper love and communion with God through his ministry and the sacraments: by baptising, celebrating Mass, hearing confessions, visiting the sick and dying, presiding at a wedding, conducting a funeral (and that can be all in a day's work – c'mon Spiderman and Ironman, keep up). The priest is invited to some of the most profound and important moments of a person's life to heal, bless, sanctify, redeem, as Jesus the High Priest works through him, despite the priest's own brokenness.

> Who then is the priest? He is the defender of truth, who stands with angels, gives glory with archangels, causes sacrifices to rise to the altar on high, shares Christ's priesthood, refashions creation, restores it in God's image, recreates it for the world on high and, even greater, is divinised and divinses.
>
> *St Gregory of Nazianzus*

One of my mentors was a Liverpool priest called Fr Jimmy Collins. He was a great influence on me because he was always ready to share God's light and mercy with others. He had an extraordinary healing ministry that packed churches and the Cathedral in the Liverpool Archdiocese. Everyone mattered to him as a unique, precious soul of God. He was a champion of the poor and vulnerable, helping them with both their spiritual and social needs. He was spiritual director of the Cursillo Movement in his area and author of spiritual books to open souls to God's grace. He was also a founding member of the Northern Catholic Conference, an event in the North of England, which has brought about great conversion of hearts and miracles. To me, his greatest attributes were his humility and great sense of humour in his service as a disciple of the Lord.

The essence of priesthood

The essence of priesthood is sacrifice! What makes Jesus different from the priests of the Old Testament is that rather than offering up an animal as a sacrifice to God for sins, Jesus offers his very self! And not only is He the priest who offers the sacrifice but He is also the victim: He himself is the sacrifice that takes away the sins of the world. When a man is ordained a priest in the Catholic Church he accepts the grace of God in the Sacrament of Holy Orders to become not just a priest but also a victim. Jesus is the only Mediator between God and man, but He gives the priest a share in his mediation, embracing the world and the effect of sin in the world. The priest will be there alongside people who are mourning, who are seeking forgiveness, who feel the burden of life with all the things that have been thrown at them. But he doesn't merely offer kind words and sympathy. Through his ministry he can raise up those people and unite them to new life, new hope in Christ, chiefly through the Mass and granting absolution in confession. On occasions such as being called to the bedside of a dying patient, who has been estranged from the Church for years, burdened with a serious sin, I realise in those moments God is saving a soul for all time and eternity.

The priest and the Mass

In the Mass, the priest isn't just a ceremonial host or a presenter, still less an entertainer. He stands in the place of Jesus, so that Jesus has a way of getting close to his people. The priest is clothed in vestments to show that he is not acting in his own name but in the Person of Jesus Christ the High Priest. He lends his voice, his hands, his whole self to Christ to offer the memorial of the one sacrifice of the Cross now made present. When the priest picks up the bread in his hands he does not say, 'This is Christ's Body,' but, 'This is my body.' He is lending his voice to Jesus. Repeating those words day after day the priest cannot help but realise that through Ordination Christ has made him someone who also has to give himself up for the good of the people. Just as a husband and a father hands over his life for the good of his family, so the priest united to Christ offers his life for the good of the Church. In celebrating the Mass the priest draws together all the cares, worries, problems of his people together with all of their joys, their hopes and their prayers, and unites them to the offering of Christ on Calvary.

A good example is Fr Walter Ciszek, an American Jesuit priest who smuggled himself into Communist Russia to serve God's people. In 1941, he was arrested by the Soviet secret police and spent 23 years in Stalin's prisons. Despite periods in solitary confinement, being beaten and starved, he served his fellow prisoners by saying Mass for them and offering confession, even though he knew that, if he was caught, he would face death.

> Priestly ordination is administered as a means of salvation, not for an individual man, but rather for the whole Church.
>
> *St Thomas Aquinas*

Greater works than Jesus?

Scott Hahn reflects on what Jesus meant when He said to his disciples that they 'will perform even greater works' than He did (John 14:12). One may ask, 'How is that possible? Think of the great miracles and signs Christ was responsible for!' But these are the words of Jesus himself, which means they must be true.

So how exactly would the apostles perform greater works?

They would perform baptism, which is a greater work than creation itself. They would forgive sins, which, as St Augustine said, is a greater work than raising the dead. They would celebrate Mass, which brings heaven into the midst of the world. These are divine actions. These are the greater works, and there are no greater works than these. It is for these, the sacraments, that Jesus ordained his priests.[1]

In the privacy and intimacy of the confessional, the priest will come across all sorts of human sins, some rather 'every day' sins, others more serious, but he doesn't hear those confessions of sin out of interest or to acquire information. He hears them so he can unite those sins and the sinner to the Cross of Christ. In the challenging words of Archbishop Fulton Sheen, when the priest holds out his hand and says the words of absolution it is as if his fingers are dripping with the blood of Christ. And when the priest says, 'I absolve you from your sins,' we are taken back to the Upper Room where Jesus appeared to his disciples and breathed his Holy Spirit upon them saying, 'If you forgive the sins of any, they are forgiven' (John 20:23).

> As for the proud minister, he is to be ranked with the devil. Christ's gift is not thereby profaned: what flows through Him keeps its purity, and what passes through him remains clear and reaches the fertile earth... The spiritual power of the sacrament is indeed comparable to light: those to be enlightened receive it in its purity, and if it should pass through defiled beings, it is not itself defiled.
>
> *St Augustine*

That same power and authority which Jesus gave the apostles is given to every priest at his Ordination through the 'laying

---

1. Hahn, Scott, *Many Are Called* (Doubleday Religion, 2010, New York), p. 136.

on of hands' by the Bishop. People share all sorts of problems and quite intimate details with each other when they trust one another, but the priest just isn't hearing the sins of the penitent because he is a trustworthy person or can give some good advice. Those who come to confess their sins do so with a firm conviction that this man has been changed into one who mediates and distributes the forgiveness and mercy of God: it is Christ acting through him. For example, when an angel sees a priest saying Mass they do not see the priest, they see Christ. When an angel sees a priest hearing confessions, they do not see the priest, but Christ, as is the case in all sacraments they administer.

On the fateful night of 14 April 1912, when the Titanic was sinking, Fr Thomas Byles, a priest on board, was given two opportunities to get into a lifeboat. Instead, Fr Byles chose to hear confessions and counsel those who were about to die. Accounts say he gathered people of all religions together for prayers and even baptised passengers. His place was with the people, God's people, hearing their confessions and giving them forgiveness and absolution as the ship was going down, heroically sacrificing himself to prepare them to meet their Maker.

Why does a priest give up marriage?

So, this all sounds great, but why does the Catholic Church say that most of its priests should give up the hope of marriage and family life in order to be a priest? The clue is in what we have already said about the complete self-giving of Christ on the Cross for the sake of his Body the Church. A man on his wedding day takes a solemn vow to give his life entirely for the sake of his bride and for the family that they will have. This is a natural desire for every man. Some people will say that it is unnatural to expect a man to sacrifice this desire. That's true – it isn't natural, it's supernatural! Jesus said it is a gift granted to some – not to everyone – adding: 'Let anyone accept this who can' (Mt 19:11-12).

On his Ordination day, the priest accepts not only a share in Christ's priesthood but also a share in Christ's marriage to his Bride the Church. The love which a man would show for his wife and children becomes the priest's dedication and devotedness to the Church. And let's understand the Church here not as an institution, but as the real people he dedicates and gives up his life for in his ministry– the members of Christ's Body. St Pope John Paul II described the priest as 'a man for others'. What he celebrates at the Mass he lives in his daily life, as he is blessed, broken and shared out for God's people.

> God said: They are My anointed ones, and I call them My Christs, because I have given them the office of administering Me to you, and have placed them like fragrant flowers in the mystical body of holy Church. The angel himself has no such dignity, for I have given it to those men whom I have chosen for my ministers, and whom I have appointed as earthly angels in this life.
>
> *St Catherine of Siena*

Role Models

Rev. Samuel Burke OP

We often think of miracles in terms of Damascene lights, dramatic healings and the like. But 'miracles', in the more general sense, can be something humanly unexpected worked by God's grace, rather than a direct and unmediated intervention by God. They can strike in the humdrum of everyday life; they can be slow-burn affairs, revealed over a period of time. And it has been a bit like that with my own vocation as a Dominican friar. My recent Ordination to the diaconate is nothing short of a miracle because nothing but the grace of God can really explain how it came to be.

We all need role models and I think of several priests who have certainly been that for me. For the sake of brevity, let me mention just one, and rewind to my time at university. At LSE, I studied law at the same time as working in politics. During my time as an undergraduate, our small Catholic student community were fortunate enough to have a remarkable chaplain, Fr Iain Matthew, a Discalced Carmelite. Through his gentle encouragement and holy example, I followed a path of discernment and prayer which, though I wasn't sure at the time, was destined to lead to the door of the Dominican Novitiate in Cambridge. God was moving within me as I tried to follow the path of Jesus more closely in my life. I wanted to be to others what good priests like Fr Iain had been to me: an image of the Lord, preaching the Good News! In a sense, one might say that my vocation is a miracle of Fr Iain's priesthood, conferred on him through the Sacrament of Holy Orders; a second miracle which is the fruit of his, if you like, and both by the grace of God!

Unbeknownst to me, more or less at the same time, my Austrian housemate, Xandro, was also inspired by Fr Iain to enter the seminary. Don Xandro has just been ordained a priest with the Communauté Saint Martin, currently ministering in France. In the law, we used to call this corroborating evidence!

All of this is not surprising, of course. Jesus called upon his disciples to be 'fishers of men' (Mt 4:19). If we take that call seriously, it can lead us to surprising places, even miraculous.

Rev. Samuel Burke is a Deacon and Dominican Friar of the English Province. A former Barrister and political advisor, he gives talks around the UK. He is also a trustee of the Christian Heritage Centre and Theodore House, a retreat and study centre that preserves the Stonyhurst Collection – the oldest surviving museum collection in the English-speaking world.

Funeral Leads to New Life

Fr Conrad Osterhout CFR

I received notes from the parish secretary for a funeral. The man who had died was the son-in-law of some very faithful parishioners. It seemed there was no need to ask further. Admittedly, I did not know the man. I supposed I could trust the details to a later discussion with the family.

The funeral was in the calendar and published in the local papers – visiting hours to view the body and time for Mass at St Mary's as well as place of interment at a local cemetery.

Shocking news emerged during the evening of the viewing of the body. The man we are going to bury is the son-in-law of faithful parishioners we know and love but his life was one of violence and crime. The son-in-law was known but not loved. His wife Sheila, daughter of our beloved parishioners, was married to Dan. They had been separated for eight years. Sheila fled the marriage because of Dan's illegal sale and use of drugs.

The night Sheila fled the house, Dan grabbed their two-year-old son, Tim. Sheila fled the place of violence and suffered eight long years without her only son. Living in the shelter of her parents, Sheila and they hoped for the day they would receive Tim back to his true family. Dan held him these years while continuing a life of women and drugs and violence.

199

A Catholic priest who administers the sacraments acts not on the basis of his own power or moral perfection (which unfortunately he often lacks), but rather 'in persona Christi'. Through his ordination, the transforming, healing, saving power of Christ is grafted onto him. Because a priest has nothing of his own, he is above all a servant. The distinguishing characteristic of every authentic priest, therefore, is humble astonishment at his own vocation.

YouCat, 250

Who has become a priest, not according to a legal requirement concerning bodily descent but by the power of an indestructible life.

Hebrews 7:16

Let everyone be struck with fear, the whole world tremble, and the heavens exult when Christ, the Son of the living God, is present on the altar in the hands of a priest!

St Francis of Assisi

THE SACRAMENT OF CONFIRMATION

they had! The early Christians referred to themselves simply as 'the living ones'. I had been dead and I wanted to be among the living again.

And I experienced joy – real joy. Not the 'pleasure' I got from my misguided pursuits, but something weightier – something that would still be there when I was sober. Real joy is the soul's response to an overwhelming outpouring of Love. It's what you get when you find God and realise your purpose in life. But that realisation didn't fully 'stick' in my life until I started living it out and sharing it with others, and the Sacrament of Confirmation helped me do that mightily.

In general, grace isn't something we 'feel'. We can smell flowers, taste burgers, shiver from a cold wind, but grace isn't physical, so sometimes it's not even accompanied by strong feelings – but we can know it's there because Jesus told us so. When we feel it, that's a gift to us, often to teach us something or to strengthen us. When we don't feel any consolation in prayer or from sacraments, God's asking us not to get caught up in emotion, to deepen in faith, and to prove our love for him by seeking him for his own sake, not just for the positive feelings faith can bring. All that being stated, God let me feel the grace when I was confirmed.

I remember when the bishop anointed my forehead. As he pulled his thumb away from my head I felt the grace hit me like a ton of bricks. I remember it distinctly because it wasn't a feeling I've had any other time before or since. It was the sense of getting hit with an enormous zap of power. I didn't want to laugh. I didn't want to cry. I just stood there speechless. I was supposed to say 'Amen' in response to his words, 'Be sealed with the Holy Spirit', but I could barely utter a sound.

The months after I received that sacrament I noticed an undeniable change in the way I lived out my Catholic faith. The happiness, love, purpose, and peace I had from my faith became contagious. In my junior year of high school, I made it my goal to share my faith or a Saint story with one person per day. 'Give me someone to tell about you, Lord,' was my constant prayer. I helped to start a prayer and faith sharing group, recruited people to youth ministry at my parish, godfathered a peer who was baptised, stood up for the dignity of women in the locker room, stood by those being mocked, went to pro-life marches, and, by the grace of God, I did it all in a way that was strangely 'cool'. Picture a longhaired teen guitarist in the 90s with baggy shorts talking to potheads about Jesus, with a rosary hanging from his belt. That was me.

My faith was no longer hidden from the world in the 'Upper Room' of my heart. I wore it on my shirtsleeve. And I was remembered by faculty and students years after I left high school for being a witness. I had been a shining light of faith.

It's been my goal to keep shining that light ever since... to be like the LIVING ONES who changed my life as a kid – and more, it's my goal to help others be the same. We have the best news ever. We can't keep it to ourselves.

Chris Stefanick (USA) is an international speaker, author and founder of reallifecatholic.com. Real Life Catholic's purpose is to ignite a bold, contagious faith in the heart of every Catholic in America, through media and live events. Chris' books include *Absolute Relativism* and *Joy to the World*. This story originally appeared in *Chosen: Your Journey through Confirmation*, which is an award-winning Confirmation programme for parishes available at AscensionPress.com.

Keep on Saying 'Yes'

David Payne

I very quickly discovered that 'unwrapping' my infant baptism was only the beginning of a new adult journey of faith. The Church calls baptism the 'gateway to life in the Spirit' and I soon realised that I needed a lot more help from God if I was going to walk into the new life won for me on the cross and powerfully reminded to me by a hairy ex-Hells Angel in a rather past-its-best hotel in Hertfordshire.

Despite the new flow of inner peace, despite being back at Church on Sundays, despite trying to pray everyday... I was still addicted to drugs and it was only a matter of time before I would be sucked back into a London life that would kill me in no time at all. So, in a rather humiliating way for a 26-year-old, I had to ask my mum for yet more help. After explaining my predicament to her, in a nanosecond she had the answer for me: 'You need the Holy Spirit!'

Despite spending a few years in a good Catholic school, my theology was very weak to say the least. I was very vague about the Third Person of the Trinity and needed further guidance. 'You need to go to a prayer meeting... and it just so happens there's one nearby starting a course on the Holy Spirit!' Well, the thought of going to a boring old prayer-meeting filled me with some anxiety. Seeing my concern, my mum immediately assured me that it would be full of young people and pretty girls with guitars!

I should have smelt a rat, especially when my friend and I found ourselves stumbling up the driveway of an old, dark convent. When the door opened, to our horror, we weren't greeted by pretty girls but by a huge crowd of old Irish ladies and three nuns! Before we could escape they bundled us in and placed us proudly in the front row with hymn books jammed into our hands.

For the next twenty minutes or so it was absolute murder. They sang (or at least they tried to!) out of tune 1960s folk songs and we began to get the giggles. Just as we were about to explode with the tension of the event something changed dramatically. Suddenly, these lovely old ladies who couldn't sing to save their lives began singing like angels. Beautiful harmonies filled the hall and we tangibly felt God's presence, the Holy Spirit, come with great power all around us. These lovely oldies were glowing as they sang in the Spirit.

I'd heard about this gift of the Spirit, first appearing at Pentecost in the Upper Room, taught about by St Paul and experienced throughout the history of the Church. However, I'd never witnessed it and it sent a shiver of excitement right through me. There was no doubt that these people were experiencing the power and joy of God in a way I desperately needed.

Despite the lack of young people and the very vast cultural divide, we went back the next week for more. On the fifth week of the course, my lovely small group leaders prayed a very simple and heartfelt prayer over me for a release of the Holy Spirit that I had received as a child. As they prayed, I prayed. In the depths of my being I said another life-changing 'YES': I unwrapped the mighty gift of my confirmation.

I'd been confirmed at the age of 10 but could barely remember it apart from a dim memory of a bishop slapping my cheek! On that cold February night, 16 years later the full force of that sacrament was released into the very core of my being. I was 'baptised in the Holy Spirit', an experience that I now realise should be at the very heart of our Catholic faith and something that Pope Francis is urging us all to experience.

That simple prayer had a massive effect on me (and my friend too). Within days the addiction from drugs had 'evaporated'. It was an amazing miracle. Some of my friends have had to walk out of addiction in a much slower way and some other areas of brokenness in my life are still being healed but there is no doubt that I had a deep and profound experience of the Holy Spirit that night at the hands of my lovely old, very Catholic Irish ladies!

Now several decades later I am still living in the 'echo' of that prayer for baptism in the Spirit. My confirmation is a foundation stone in my life. Of course, it's not a one-off experience. It's vital to keep the 'fires burning' through prayer, the sacraments (especially the Eucharist), reading the Bible and being part of a vibrant Christian community worshipping and serving together.

At the heart of our faith is a relationship, a daily experience of the presence, power and help of the Holy Spirit that we can experience so powerfully in the sacraments. We need to keep reminding each other that our lives were never meant to be a DIY project. We were made to be filled with God for the sake of the world!

Charisms: What are they? Who are they for? What does the Church teach?

Ralph Martin

Part 1

Rediscovering the charismatic dimension: recent magisterial teaching

St Pope John Paul II stated that one of the most significant contributions of the Second Vatican Council was the 'rediscovery' of the 'charismatic dimension' of the Church.

During the feast of Pentecost, in 1998, the Pope asked representatives of all the renewal movements of the Church to join with him to celebrate this feast. Over 500,000 people from more than 50 different movements came. What the Pope did was to gather together the teaching of Scripture and Vatican II, on the charismatic gifts of the Spirit and proclaim them with urgency and passion. He begins:

> The Church's self-awareness (is) based on the certainty that Jesus Christ is alive, is working in the present and changes life... With the Second Vatican Council, the Comforter

recently gave the Church... a renewed Pentecost, instilling a new and unforeseen dynamism.

Whenever the Spirit intervenes, he leaves people astonished. He brings about events of amazing newness; he radically changes persons and history. This was the unforgettable experience of the Second Vatican Ecumenical Council during which, under the guidance of the same Spirit, the Church rediscovered the charismatic dimension as one of her constitutive elements: 'It is not only through the sacraments and the ministrations of the Church that the Holy Spirit makes holy the people, leads them and enriches them with his virtues. Allotting his gifts according as he wills (see 1 Corinthians 12:11), he also distributes special graces among the faithful of every rank... He makes them fit and ready to undertake various tasks and offices for the renewal and building up of the Church.' (*Lumen Gentium*, 12)

With these words St Pope John Paul II honestly acknowledged what many theologians, Scripture scholars and Church historians had demonstrated in their studies, that the charismatic workings of the Holy Spirit are an essential and complementary reality to the working of the Spirit in the sacramental and hierarchical dimensions of the Church's existence. The Pope also honestly acknowledged that the charismatic dimension, important as it was, was nevertheless in a way forgotten, or overshadowed by perhaps a too exclusive emphasis on the sacramental and hierarchical, and it required a special action of the Holy Spirit in the Second Vatican Council to bring the Church back to an awareness of the importance of this 'constitutive' dimension.

The Pope in his speech went on to make this explicit:

> The institutional and charismatic aspects are co-essential as it were to the Church's constitution. They contribute, although differently, to the life, renewal and sanctification of God's People. It is from this providential rediscovery of the Church's charismatic dimension that before and after the Council, a remarkable pattern of growth has been established for ecclesial movements and new communities… You present here, are the tangible proof of this 'outpouring' of the Spirit.

Pope Emeritus Benedict XVI in one of the first initiatives of his pontificate convened a similar gathering of the movements in the Church in 2006 and reaffirmed the teaching of St Pope John Paul II, quoting his remarks on this occasion.

St John Paul II, as does Benedict XVI, cites the foundational document of Vatican II, the Constitution on the Church, 12 (*Lumen Gentium*, 12) as the basis for this teaching. The background to this particular text is of significance. There was a debate among the council fathers about whether the Church still needed the 'charismatic dimension' and in particular, the charismatic gifts, today, or whether they were intended just for the early Church to help her get established. The argument went that these workings of the Spirit were needed to help get the Church going but now that we had sacraments and hierarchy they were no longer needed. This argument did not carry the day, as there is no basis in Scripture for believing that this important dimension is only needed for a while. In fact the Scripture witnesses to just the opposite; the charismatic gifts are an important accompaniment to the preaching of the Gospel and the health of the internal life of the Church. The council fathers voted overwhelmingly to affirm this truth and accept the text that St John Paul II cites.

This Conciliar affirmation of the importance of the charismatic dimension was a way of affirming a dynamic vision of lay participation in the life of the Church and is closely linked to the important affirmations of the 'universal call to holiness' and the 'universal call to mission'.

Biblical foundations

While St John Paul II quoted the Council text as a basis for his teaching, the Council text itself cites the Bible as the foundation of its teaching. What is the Biblical teaching about the 'charismatic dimension' and 'charisms'? The particular text that the Council cites is 1 Corinthians 12:11:

> But one and the same Spirit produces all of these, distributing them individually to each person as he wishes.

The 'all of these' that this text references are mentioned in the previous verses:

> Now in regard to spiritual gifts [charisms], brothers, I do not want you to be unaware... To each individual the manifestation of the Spirit is given for some benefit. To one is given through the Spirit the expression of wisdom; to another the expression of knowledge according to the same Spirit; to another faith by the same Spirit; to another gifts of healing by the one Spirit; to another mighty deeds; to another prophecy; to another discernment of spirits; to another varieties of tongues; to another interpretation of tongues. (1 Corinthians 12:1, 7-10)

But this isn't the only list of charisms that we find in the New Testament. There are also lists in Romans 12, 1 Peter 4, and Ephesians 4. We only have space to look at one of these additional lists and it will be the one in Romans 12:

> For as in one body we have many parts, and all the parts do not have the same function, so we, though many, are one body in Christ and individually parts of one another. Since we have gifts that differ according to the grace given to us, let us exercise them: if prophecy, in proportion to the faith; if ministry, in ministering; if one is a teacher, in teaching; if one exhorts, in exhortation; if one contributes,

in generosity; if one is over others, with diligence; if one does acts of mercy, with cheerfulness. Let love be sincere; hate what is evil, hold on to what is good; love one another with mutual affection; anticipate one another in showing honour. Do not grow slack in zeal, be fervent in spirit, serve the Lord. Rejoice in hope, endure in affliction, persevere in prayer. Contribute to the needs of the holy ones, exercise hospitality. (Romans 12: 4-13)

In this text, as in the 1 Corinthians 12 text, the context for the explanation of the charisms is in understanding the Church as a 'body' with different members, all playing different roles, all essential for the overall well-being of the body. Sometimes the statement is made that Paul clearly says that love is more important than the charisms, and that is certainly true. The beautiful hymn to love in 1 Corinthians 13 is sandwiched between two chapters that contain important teaching on the charisms. But Paul is not presenting a 'cafeteria approach to Christianity'. He isn't pitting charisms and charity against each other. As a matter of fact, he sees the acceptance and exercise of spiritual gifts as, precisely, an important way of loving. He summarises his teaching like this: 'Pursue love, but strive eagerly for the spiritual gifts, especially that you may prophesy' (1 Corinthians 14:1). It's not a matter of either or, but both and. Love is certainly primary – more important than charisms if you will – but the charisms are given by the

Spirit to help us to love and serve in specific ways that are important for the well-being of the Church. Paul's advice is to 'make love our aim' and to eagerly pursue the spiritual gifts. We see the same harmony between love, holiness and the faithful exercise of charisms in the passage from Romans cited above. Charisms aren't isolated gifts but are interwoven with the life of love, service, and mission which characterises the very nature of the Church. This is why St John Paul II calls the charismatic dimension and the institutional dimension 'co-essential' to the Church's constitution. It's not either sacraments and hierarchy or charisms; it's both. Both are essential to the healthy function of Church life and when these elements are not in right relationship with each other the Church is weakened.

The *Catechism of the Catholic Church* reflects the biblical, conciliar and papal teaching in its numerous mentions of charisms:

> Whether extraordinary or simple and humble, charisms are graces of the Holy Spirit which directly or indirectly benefit the Church, ordered as they are to her building up, to the good of men and to the needs of the world. (CCC 799)

> Charisms are to be accepted with gratitude by the person who receives them, and by all members of the Church as well. They are a wonderfully rich grace for the apostolic

again. It seemed she was healed and now she didn't need an operation after all! I was shocked. I certainly hadn't had faith for this, but she accepted it quite naturally. I remember telling a fellow journalist about this some years later. She wanted to know if I had the paperwork and concrete evidence to back this story up. But I don't. When these things happen in your everyday life, you don't think about proving it, because the evidence is before you.

In the same way I believe that there are many such healings going on all around us through God's action and the power of the Holy Spirit. These are usually only known among a person's network of friends and family. They have no interest in having an officially recognised healing as such. They are just glad to get their health and their life back. The stories I now tell are these kinds of healings. They have not been rigorously investigated or researched, but I know they are true because I have been part of the story or have interviewed the person concerned and seen the evidence in their life.

Roberto, one good friend of mine, has had several healings over the course of his remarkable life. A former boxing champion, he suffered brain damage as a result of the blows he received in the ring. When he was in his twenties he was suddenly struck down, and for a year lay in a hospital bed with locked-in syndrome. He could hear and see, but he couldn't move or speak. The doctors said he would never talk or walk again and would be a permanent invalid. His mother, a devout

Orthodox Christian, went to Corfu where she came from. Here she prayed at the tomb of St Spiridon, the patron saint of the island, who was known to be a great intercessor for healing and miracles. She was a simple woman, but she had a close relationship with Jesus and trusted him implicitly, believing that God would hear her petition for her son. We, in the secular West, can sometimes dismiss these examples of popular religiosity but the Lord sees the heart and the charism of faith behind them, and her prayers were answered.

Shortly afterwards, Roberto for the first time, started to respond to the therapy that he was being given. The doctors were unable to explain why this was happening, as clinically this should have been impossible. This was not an instant healing, but one which involved years of painstaking therapy and rehab-ilitation as Roberto learnt to walk and talk again. Thirty years later Roberto, although he is still registered disabled, is able to lead a more or less normal life. The doctors have no explanation of why this has been possible as MRI scans show that his condition has not changed.

Roberto's physical healing also went alongside a religious and moral conversion too. In his former life, he was involved in a lot of criminal activity, but in the year 1999, following a deep encounter with Jesus, he returned to the practice of his Catholic faith in a very committed way. In gratitude for all that God has done for him, he feels called to live a life of service to the Church and the wider community. He is very aware that it is God who has healed him and him alone who sustains him. Thus he avails himself of all the sacraments that the Church has to offer on a regular basis. He receives the Eucharist daily, goes to confession once a week and receives the sacrament of the sick, at a monthly healing service in his parish, at St Mary's in Croydon. He also has received deliverance prayer on several occasions from priests involved in this often little-understood ministry. This has helped to deliver him from the negative spiritual effects of the dark forces in which he was involved in his past life of violence as well as alcoholism and drug addiction. This ministry, he says, has helped bring him great emotional freedom and spiritual liberation.

As if this was not enough, the Lord has continued to perform other significant healings in his life, which I have been witness to. One was about seven years ago, when he came to help me manning a stall at a Catholic Miracle Rally in London organised by the Cor et Lumen Christi community. Roberto shouldn't really have been there because he was in great pain with his knee, which was badly swollen and inflamed. He had recently been to the doctor to have his knee syringed of blood and fluid and his GP had decided that surgery was now needed to remedy the situation. This had happened with his other knee, some years previously. A date was thus set for a few weeks later at the local hospital.

We had been busy over the lunch break and were about to go off and eat, when I suggested to Roberto that we pop into the hall for a short while to see what was going on. Damian Stayne, who was leading the service, was praying for an outpouring of the Holy Spirit. Many people in the hall were speaking in tongues, which is a special prayer language mentioned in the Bible. As I work for the Charismatic Renewal, this was something quite commonplace for me, and after ten minutes or so, as I was hungry, I suggested that we leave and go and have a cup of tea. Roberto didn't say anything at the time. Later, however, he told me that he had felt very dizzy as people had prayed, and he had felt the power of the Holy Spirit strongly in the room. It was only the next day that he realised he had no more pain in his knee and that he could bend it and walk on it as normal again.

He decided he would still attend his hospital appointment to witness to his healing to the doctors and tell them that he didn't need the operation any more. Rather than dismissing what he said, it turned out that both doctors were women of faith. One was a Christian and the other a Muslim. They both rejoiced with him, saying 'God can do anything He wants,' without insisting on taking another X-ray or going ahead with the operation. All I can say is that seven years later I can testify that Roberto's knee is still fine.

Kristina Cooper (UK) is a speaker, journalist and editor of *GoodNews Magazine*, a magazine for Catholic Charismatic Renewal (CCR) in the UK and Ireland, a resource for those who are keen to grow in their spiritual journey.

Confirmation

Editor with Kristina Cooper

When I was studying to be a priest some of the guys in the seminary thought it would be a good idea to go down to the local pub for their karaoke night. Now just because we were seminarians did not mean our decision-making was always good. The part of the night that did it for me was when some of the lads after a few drinks got up on the karaoke and started singing *Sister Act* songs. Now I'm from a showbiz background, but even that was way too camp for me! During the evening, there was a table close to us with a mixture of men and women who found out we were training to be priests, and kept giving us banter. I say banter, but some of the words they used aren't even in the dictionary. We were giving as good as we got – with words from the dictionary – and it was a friendly/fun atmosphere. One of these ladies approached me – she was about 40, dark hair, attractive. She was insistent that we should sing a duet together; I was insistent we shouldn't. So, the amusement carried on throughout the course of the night.

But near the end of the night I felt inspired to give this lady a miraculous medal. (It's something I heard St Teresa of Kolkata did; whenever she felt inspired, she would give out miraculous medals.) So I gave one to her and explained it was an image of Our Lady and that this was a sign of her love and blessings for her from heaven. She looked at me and said, 'You can't give me this.' I replied, 'Why not?' She said, 'Because you don't know the things I've done in my life.' And in that moment I felt God's love for her. 'I don't want to judge you, I just want to bless you,' I told her. And to this day I'll never forget what came next: her eyes filled up with tears and she hugged me and walked off clutching her medal.

What does the Holy Spirit do in the life of a believer?

I believe that the ability, the power, to evangelise comes from this sacrament – the Sacrament of Confirmation. Confirmation enables us to take up Jesus' commission to love one another as He has loved us (John 15:12) with the same love that He and the Father shared (John 17:26). Jesus does not give us a commission without the means to carry it out. To be an effective Christian we need supernatural gifts and supernatural powers.

> Holiness consists simply in doing God's will, and being just what God wants us to be.
>
> *St Thérèse of Lisieux*

Confirmation is the sacrament of 'discipleship'. After Jesus' ascension, we are told that the apostles were scared, frightened individuals hiding in an upper room. At Pentecost, however, everything changed for them! They became fearless, merciful and courageous evangelists and teachers of the faith, ready to serve God at any cost. At confirmation, Pentecost happens for us! That's what the Church teaches in the *Catechism*: in confirmation, the grace of, Pentecost is made present and there is a full outpouring of the Holy Spirit (CCC 1302). As Dr Tim Gray notes, the power of Pentecost is unleashed again on the whole world when the Sacrament of Confirmation takes place. Just as the apostles received a power they did not have **naturally** to witness to the Gospel, so too those who are confirmed receive *super*-**natural** power to fulfil the same great commission to go out and evangelise:

> But you shall receive power when the Holy Spirit has come upon you; and you shall be my witnesses in Jerusalem and in all Judea and Samaria and to the end of the earth. (Acts 1:8)

The Greek word for witness is *martyras*, from which we get the English word 'martyr'. Dr Tim Gray again teaches us that it is not within our human strength to witness to Christ and the Gospel. We need to 'die to our self' and that is not natural for us. It is only through the Holy Spirit, Christ's Spirit within us, that we can do that. Disciples who are not afraid of anything standing in the way of their witness and proclamation of the Gospel, not even death, are very dangerous disciples indeed. They will lead many to God because they know that they can do all things through the One who gives them strength (Philippians 4:13).

The Greek word for strength is *dynami/s* from which we get the English word 'dynamite'. This is a mighty explosion of love which God gives us so we can fearlessly proclaim his Kingdom. He will not leave us orphans (i.e. relying only on our own devices) to carry out his plans (John 14:18). For years I used to run away from even the thought of ever being able to evangelise. Whenever the idea about becoming a priest came to mind, my excuse was that I was not able to evangelise: 'What? Speak about Christ and his love? I wouldn't be able to string two sentences together!' But I learnt that it is the Holy Spirit that does it if we give him permission and surrender to his 'dynamite' power.

When I was still in show business, I was once in a production with a famous TV and movie actress. During the season we had some profound conversations about God and his love. A few months after the production finished I woke up one morning and felt inspired to pray for her. During the prayer I was prompted to send her a text message to let her know I was praying for her and her family. I wasn't expecting the text message I got back. She said she had woken up that morning and said to God, 'If you're out there looking after me, show me a sign'... and then my text arrived.

Both the *Catechism* and the *Code of Canon Law* underline that confirmation is a sacrament of strengthening. It strengthens an individual's relationship with Jesus, then it strengthens his or her ability to go out and proclaim and defend the faith as witnesses of Christ and his Cross and Resurrection.

Who can be a true disciple?

Think of all the incredible witnesses that have been true disciples over the years: St Pope John Paul II, St Teresa of Kolkata, St Francis of Assisi, etc. – all ordinary men and women who allowed God to impact their hearts and set them on fire with his love so they could share his love with others. God gave them a new strength to witness and spread the faith in word but also in action, through love. The world has known many influential leaders, many great scientists,

> But it is God who establishes us with you in Christ, and has commissioned us; he has put his seal upon us and given us his Spirit in our hearts as a guarantee.
>
> *2 Corinthians 1:21-22*

discoverers, artists and actors, but they are not remembered as lovingly or as fondly as the saints. Why? Because the saints did it with love – not a normal, natural, everyday kind of love, but an endless, eternal love. They tapped into the heart of God himself. Through the power of God's Holy Spirit they not only received the capacity to love way beyond their own limitations, but they were given special gifts and qualities which are also available to us in the Sacrament of Confirmation, such as:

1. an increase of our baptismal grace
2. growth in a deeper relationship with God and knowing him as 'Abba Father' (Romans 8:15)
3. becoming more united to Christ

4. an increase in the gifts of the Holy Spirit and strengthening our bond with the Church.

As that famous song ('I Got Rhythm') goes, 'Who could ask for anything more?' An example I once heard explains what happens: imagine you have a glass of milk (that represents you), and then you put some chocolate powder into it (that represents your baptism). Well now the chocolate powder is lying at the bottom of the glass. But when it is stirred up (your confirmation) all the gifts are mixed up and rise to the surface. You become who you are as a new creation in Christ!

Your mission?

It's simple. We were meant to set the world on fire. Did you realise that? My favourite saint, Catherine of Siena, believed 'If you are what you are meant to be, you will set the whole world on fire!' There's a story of a person dying and going to heaven and he meets Jesus face-to-face. Jesus takes him into a room where there is a beautiful treasure chest. The person asks if he can look in the chest. Jesus says, 'Of course!' The person opens it up and is blown away by what he sees inside: all these amazing gifts, graces and talents! He says, 'Wow, these are amazing. Whose are they?' Jesus says, 'Yours. But you never used them when you were on earth.'

> And no one can say 'Jesus is Lord' except by the Holy Spirit.
>
> *1 Corinthians 12:3*

Blessed Pope Paul VI told us that 'the Church exists to evangelise' and Bishop Robert Barron adds, 'The Church exists to produce saints.' Do you see the connection? The effective workers in the harvest are God's chosen ones. That includes you! History has shown that a watered-down, rather apologetic manner in mentioning your faith to others is never what the Holy Spirit had in mind. That won't attract anyone, so the Spirit supplies us with supernatural gifts we are meant to grow in, and even excel at, particularly ones such as wisdom, understanding, knowledge, fortitude, piety, counsel, and fear of the Lord (which is 'reverential awe' of him, not being afraid of him!). As you can see from these amazing gifts, if the most important gift you volunteer to your parish community is calling out the bingo numbers, you're overqualified!!

Of course, the supernatural gifts we have been given in baptism which were strengthened in confirmation need to be developed, something which happens gradually the more we surrender areas of our lives to God. One man who had been encouraged to attend a Life in the Spirit seminar – a course which encourages people to give their lives to Jesus in a deeper way and be open to the gifts of the Holy Spirit – was told that a key moment in the seminar was when people were prayed with for the release of the spiritual gifts. He was very excited about this, but was extremely disappointed when he felt nothing after this 'special' prayer. He expected something sensational to happen. A week or so later he was complaining about this to his wife: 'Nothing has happened to me.' 'What do you mean nothing has happened to you?' she asked. 'You've stopped swearing and become a daily Mass-goer!'

Sometimes God can be at work in our lives and we are not even aware of the changes because we are focussing on feelings, while others see our outward behaviour and the changes in us.

There's always more!

A friend of mine was once involved with preparing teenagers for confirmation. She and the team took the candidates and sponsors on a weekend retreat. The retreat team did a fantastic job and afterwards when my friend was discussing with the young people how they felt about it one girl said, 'Now that I understand what it means to make a commitment to Christ and to be a Christian, I am not sure if I want to make that step.' What upset my friend, however, was not that she said this, but that the girl still went ahead and wanted to be confirmed because she didn't see that it had anything to do with being a disciple of Christ. It was just something cultural, a rite of passage, to please her parents. She's now calling out bingo numbers in her local parish church...

But seriously, there is a challenge here. Were the Saints any more special or extraordinary than you or me? No. It was the Holy Spirit within them! They discovered this key to holiness by surrendering to the Spirit. Through this they not only changed but they transformed the societies in which they lived. To return to the inspiring words of St Catherine, they were set on fire with God's love (which is the Holy Spirit) in order to set the world on fire.

To be a saint is not easy. It never has been. But we don't do it alone. As St Patrick said, it is 'through him (Christ) and with him and in him'. We take our lead from Jesus and how He evangelised and ministered to others. After all, if we share in his Spirit and are now God's adopted sons and daughters, his mission is our mission. The supernatural gifts I already mentioned were part of Jesus' ministry and outreach to sinners. But He also used what the Church calls 'charisms' (special graces). Ralph Martin, the Catholic evangelist and writer, goes into more detail about these in his contribution to this book and about St Paul's teaching. Let me just touch on a couple of them:

> We can study the whole history of salvation, we can study the whole of Theology, but without the Spirit we cannot understand. It is the Spirit that makes us realise the truth or – in the words of Our Lord – it is the Spirit that makes us know the voice of Jesus.
>
> *Pope Francis*

In the same way that Jesus 'knew' about the life/background of the Samaritan woman at the well, saints such as Jean Vianney and Padre Pio 'knew' about sins that had not been confessed by penitents in the Sacrament of Reconciliation. How? By the gift/charism of prophecy. And just as Jesus healed people, saints such as Martin of Porres and John of God, who were Religious brothers and not medical doctors, were able to miraculously cure people from life-threatening conditions through that supernatural gift of the Spirit, the gift/charism of healing. From the Gospels we read that Jesus 'knew' what was in the hearts of his hearers. Similarly, saints such as Catherine of Siena were given the ability to 'know' exactly what to say to others to bring them to conversion through the gift/charism of the word of knowledge.

The Time of Mercy

I believe the times we are living in are times are great grace and mercy when God is doing amazing things and wants to pour out his abundant blessings and miraculous love. Why do I believe this? Because as Tertullian said, 'The blood of the martyrs is the seed of the Church.' In the twentieth century, there were more Christian martyrs than all the other centuries put together. And since the turn of the twenty-first century, the writer John Allen claims there have already been one million Christian martyrs. I believe their blood and their sacrifice for the Gospel is the source of great graces and miracles for these times in which we live, which is why it is a time of mercy. Pope Francis himself, before calling for the Year of Mercy, said that this had been on the heart of St John Paul II for a number of years. Why is it a time of mercy, a time of great grace and blessing? The author and theologian Fr Michael Gaitley reflects that it is because the era in which we live is so dark and evil. In the Bible we see that in times of great darkness and calamity God provides even greater blessings and grace. St Paul puts it like this: 'Where sin increased, grace abounded all the more' (Romans 5:20). Are we ready to receive all God's grace and mercy so we can be ambassadors and carriers of it?

How much Holy Spirit do you want?

Like St Augustine, the early Church fathers believed it was a matter of faith and desire. St Cyril of Jerusalem used an example of a tree that puts forth fruit from its branches when it is watered. Similarly, he said, souls bear the fruit of holiness when contrition for their sins has made them worthy of receiving the Holy Spirit. St Basil the Great put it this way: 'The power of the Spirit fills the whole universe, but He gives himself to only those who are worthy, acting in each according to his faith.' St Irenaeus realised these gifts were important and beneficial for the building up of the Church and its members

> Create in me a clean heart, O God, and put a new and right spirit within me.
>
> *Psalm 51:12*

when he observed: 'We hear many of the brethren in the Church having prophetic charisms and speaking all kinds of tongues through the Spirit; and bringing the secrets of men to light for their good, and expounding the mysteries of God.'

In order for faith to increase it has to be given away. When you give, you receive. The more we witness to our faith and speak about it, the greater the gift of faith grows in us. After all, a flower blooms beautifully when it is exposed to the light, not when it's hidden away in a cupboard. When I was in seminary, a visiting priest, Fr Stephen Wang, gave a retreat and he said something that changed my perspective on evangelising ever since. Simply, he remarked: 'Get used to failing for Jesus, because the more you fail, the less you will be afraid of taking risks for him.' Why? His power is made perfect in our weakness (2 Corinthians 12:9) and we learn to rely on him.

The Church teaches us that the principal agent of evangelisation is the Holy Spirit, and the way in which we grow in deeper love and union with God is through the Holy Spirit. As Fr Cantalamessa says, 'God has only one response to our prayers: He sends us the Holy Spirit.' That was evident even before I became a priest. I went on holiday to LA with my brother and some friends. We were in the Hollywood Boulevard area when we decided to break up, do our own thing and meet up later in the day. I took myself off down a couple of streets, turned a corner and came face-to-face with a homeless man. At that time, I had been working with homeless people back in my hometown, Rochdale, and one of the things that the homeless taught me was that they don't always need food and drink, sometimes

> For you did not receive the spirit of slavery to fall back into fear, but you have received the spirit of sonship. When we cry 'Abba! Father!' it is the Spirit himself bearing witness with our spirit that we are children of God, and if children, then heirs, heirs of God and fellow heirs with Christ, provided we suffer with him so that we may also be glorified with him.
>
> *Romans 8:15-17*

they just want a smile, a friendly conversation. So, I chatted with this man for a little while before shaking his hand and wishing him a good day. As I walked away from him down the street, the alarm on my watch went off to let me know it was three o' clock, reminding me to say the Divine Mercy 'Three O' Clock Prayer' (I have a devotion to the Divine Mercy). So I said the prayer and at the end added: 'God, today my intention is for that homeless man, that he may know how loved he is by you.' And from the depths of my being I heard an inner voice say, 'Why don't you tell him?' I stopped. Then, realising what had happened, I tried to respond in the holiest way I could. 'No! No! That's not what I prayed for. It was for you to tell him not me.' And the same voice spoke again: 'If you don't tell him, who will?' I knew I had to go back, so – saying a prayer for guidance and strength – I went up to him and said, 'Hi, how you doing?' He replied, 'You were just here.' I said, 'I know. I have something I have to tell you. I've never done this before, but I need to say it…' I paused, and then continued, 'Jesus loves you.' There was a moment of silence, his eyes began to water and he said, 'You're the second person today to say that to me.'

That man taught me that evangelisation and loving others isn't about getting caught up in your own insecurities, anxieties and fears, but saying 'Yes' to Jesus and letting him do the rest. And what was the way I was able to say yes? By tapping into my confirmation promises and praying, 'Come Holy Spirit.'

Led by the Hand of God

Jeff Cavins

I grew up in the 60s and 70s when the Catholic Church was experiencing dramatic changes after Vatican II. By the time I reached the age of confirmation, I was woefully lacking in the basic understanding of the faith. I do however recall that day in May of 1971 when I was confirmed and received a Bible as a gift. I was intrigued by this gift and held it in awe, figuring at some point in my life I would try to understand it. My brilliant idea was to read one verse a day in hopes of finishing it when I was old with a full understanding of the holy book. My plan only lasted a few weeks, however. The Bible remained on my bed stand for a few years until we moved to a new house several miles away.

Five years later, inspired by a Protestant family that read the Bible a lot, I bought a leather Bible and began to read it with great excitement. Over the years, that led me to teaching the Bible Timeline, a method of understanding the Scriptures by following 14 narratives in the books in the Bible that follow the story of salvation. Eventually I developed several Bible study courses. One evening while I was attending a volunteers' thank-you dinner for small group leaders of a local Bible study that I had been teaching, I mentioned to the group that I would be leading a pilgrimage to the Holy Land and for those interested, I sent around a sheet of paper. When the paper made the rounds and returned to my table, the gentleman next to me jotted down his address.

I couldn't believe it! He lived in my boyhood home! 'My parents built that house!' I exclaimed. Then I asked him if he wouldn't mind if I came to his house to see it. He was very generous and offered for the whole family to visit, including my parents and sisters. A few rooms still had the decorations my mother had made. I asked if he wouldn't mind if I saw my old room.

'Sure,' he replied. 'Which room is it?'

'It's the first one down the hall to the left,' I said pointing.

'Oh, that room is now my office,' he said, leading us all down the hall.

As I peered into that familiar room, I gasped. There, where my bed stand used to be holding my confirmation Bible, now stood a whole display case with all of the Bible studies I had produced. We were all amazed.

I was so blessed to see the tangible results of the anointing of the Holy Spirit at confirmation. That drawing by the Holy Spirit to read the Bible, which began at confirmation, grew into a library of studies now sitting on a shelf in the same location.

Jeff Cavins (USA) is an international speaker and creator of *The Great Adventure: A Journey through the Bible* – a practical, useful, interactive Bible timeline system. Currently being used in parishes across North America. For six years, Jeff produced and hosted EWTN's *Life on the Rock* and is currently the host of Relevant Radio's drive time show *Morning Air.* Jeff is also the editor and writer of Catholic Scripture Study along with Scott Hahn, Mark Shea and others, available weekly at CatholicExchange.com.

Life to the Full

Jenny Baker

The nuns that taught me at school would never have put their money on me working for the Church. I was not the most accommodating student and mucked around at any given opportunity. I was brought up within a loving, devout Catholic family but like so many young people my teenage years had enticed me into a lapsed mindset and although I did believe in God, I didn't ever expect him to impact my life.

I made my confirmation at the age of 11. The first of two most vivid memories of making this sacrament was my dress. In those days, we wore white with a veil just like First Holy Communion. There was great 'debate' between my parents, as my mother had spent so much on the dress that came from an expensive store in London. I, needless to say, loved it! The other memory is of my confirmation sponsor. We were told to invite someone who would be a good role model of prayer. I knew that was my Granny. When she came to stay, my younger sister had to vacate her bed and Granny would come and sleep in my room with me. I was always intrigued by the ritual of prayer that took place when she came up to bed. I would be waiting under my bedcovers fighting sleep as she undressed and placed her stockings in the shape of a cross at the end of the bed; this, she assured me, would be where her guardian angel sat overnight and kept watch. She would then switch out the light, climb into bed, take out her rosary beads and light up a cigarette! As a child, I delighted in the click of the rosary beads and the attempt to stay awake until the glow of her cigarette was put out, I never managed it.

What do I remember about the teaching of the Holy Spirit from the confirmation catechesis I was given? Not much. I did understand that I had received the Holy Spirit through my baptism and He had been strengthened in me through my confirmation, but I had no idea of the miraculous new life He brings if we are open and expectant. Sadly, it took until I was grown up, married with children of my own, to come to this realisation.

Having given birth to twin daughters I went back to the Church to have them baptised. However, although I made this commitment and took my Sunday obligation fairly seriously, due to family bereavement and circumstances of life, I started to question why I was bringing my children up as Catholics. Did I really believe?

I became friends with a mum whose daughter was the same age as my girls; others described her as a committed Christian. This was an interesting comment I thought, as although I went to Church, people would not say the same about me. Intrigued, I asked her about her faith and she spoke about her relationship with God and she even mentioned Jesus! She told me they were running an Alpha course at her Anglican Church and invited me to come along. I had never thought of going to anything 'religious' before and the idea filled me with dread, but someone (little did I know it was the Holy Spirit) was enticing me to go.

The way I would describe the Alpha course was like doing a jigsaw puzzle, week by week different pieces began to come together and I realised that I had buried so much of what I had known as a child.

Halfway through the course we were invited to go on a retreat weekend to look at the person and the work of the Holy Spirit. At the beginning, I was so sure that I wouldn't be going on the weekend, but as time went on I felt more and more drawn to go. The retreat brought a new revelation of the power and work of God in my life. Having heard a talk about how the Holy Spirit pours the love of God the Father into our hearts and how He can bring us to a new encounter with Jesus, I was offered the opportunity to be prayed with. I remember being very hesitant about this. No one had ever offered to pray with me before, they had offered to say a prayer for me or light a candle, but this was a new thing. This was someone being willing to stand with me and intercede on my behalf to the Father and ask him to refresh me in the love of the Holy Spirit – this was so different. I recognised in that moment how much I needed God and that life with a diluted understanding of who He was, was not enough. I accepted the offer of prayer and nervously opened my hands and heart to God who was just waiting to enter in. This was a miraculous moment, a simple and gentle moment in time, which changed my life and the life of my family. I would describe it as the realisation of my baptism and my confirmation; I had always known deep down that I had received something in these sacraments; it was as if I had been given a gift and I had put it away in a cupboard thinking that one day, when I am older, wiser, had more time, I would take it out and examine it further. This was the time that I opened the cupboard door and unwrapped the gift I had been given through the sacraments.

I now realise the grace of the sacraments is always available to us but we have to say 'Yes' to fully come alive in our faith and experience the fullness of all God wants for us. This is a daily choice which leads to a life of miracles.

Jenny Baker (UK) is a speaker who travels around the UK and beyond to address parishes and conferences. She has helped develop and present the CaFE resources along with David Payne. She is Vice Chair of the English National Service Committee (NSC) for Catholic Charismatic Renewal. And she is the coordinator for the Celebrate conferences around the country.

Charisms: What are they? Who are they for? What does the Church teach?

Ralph Martin

Part 2

Before we go any further we need to understand better what charisms are. Charisms are not just 'natural abilities' but gifts distributed by the Spirit to each person as He wills. Charisms often build on and work with our natural personalities and abilities, but not always.

This is clearly the case in the more obvious 'supernatural' gifts such as healing or miracles. When someone who has been given the charism of healing prays with people who are sick, many more get well than when people without that particular gift pray for the sick. We all should pray for the sick but some who pray for the sick have a special gift of healing working through them. The action of the Holy Spirit is also present in the less obviously supernatural charisms.

We are grateful for all our preachers and teachers but some seem to have a special 'gift' that is not only the fruit of human eloquence or diligent study but brings with it a sense of God's presence and has a particular ability to help us recognise that the Lord is present and speaking to us in the preaching or teaching. Sometimes we call this exercise of the Word 'anointed'. The charism of 'prophecy' in the broad sense or the charism of teaching is then at work. Prophecy in this sense isn't about particular predictions, although this may happen occasionally as well. It's rather about Spirit-inspired speaking of God's Word that causes the heart of the hearers to 'burn' similar to what the disciples on the road to Emmaus experienced when Jesus explained the Scriptures to them.

The same is true with the gift of encouragement or exhortation. We are grateful for 'positive personalities' that lift up relationships but there are certain people who seem to have a particular gift for speaking the right word at the right time, words of encouragement, that lift us up in a special way, so that we may experience the impartation of grace, peace, or hope that we need.

The same is true with the gift of 'generous giving'. We are grateful for all those who give generously to support the work of the Church and its ministries – and we all should be doing this – but there are certain among us who God has gifted to be able to make money and in being able to discern what, where, when and to whom to give it, in a way that is truly remarkable. Some have a 'gift/charism' of giving generously, the right amount at the right time to the right recipient.

It also seems clear from the Scripture that each member of the body is given some charism or charisms, that each member of the body has a call or vocation, to use the gifts they are given to build up the body and help carry out the Church's mission. It also seems clear that none of the scriptural lists of charisms we have cited intend to be comprehensive in listing the possible charisms. They are rather indicative of the rich diversity of gifts that the Holy Spirit gives, not all of which are listed or perhaps ever could be.

There has been a lot of attention given to the call for the laity to 'fully, actively and consciously' participate in the Liturgy, but attention also needs to be given to the need for lay people to recognise the gift(s) that they are being given by the Spirit that they have a responsibility to exercise, in love, for the good of the Church.

Witness of the Tradition

The teaching of the contemporary magisterium is not only supported by the clear biblical teaching but illumined by the early tradition of the Church. A great deal of helpful scholarship has been done which illumines the experience of the Spirit and the charisms in the first centuries of the Church.[1]

---

1. Fr George Montague and Fr Killian McDonnell have written a major work tracing the biblical and historical experience of the Spirit in relationship to the sacraments of Christian initiation. Their major work is: *Christian Initiation and Baptism in the Holy Spirit* (Collegeville: The Liturgical Press, A Michael Glazier Book, 1991). They have written a much shorter, popular summary of their work from which the citations in this article are taken: *Fanning the Flame: What does Baptism in the Holy*

Tertullian, in his *On Baptism*, written in the early third century, addresses the newly baptised who are about to enter the area where all will celebrate the Eucharist:

> Therefore, you blessed ones, for whom the grace of God is waiting, when you come up from the most sacred bath of the new birth, when you spread out your hands for the first time in your mother's house (the church) with your brethren, ask your Father, ask your Lord, for the special gift of his inheritance, the distribution of charisms, which form an additional, underlying feature (of baptism). 'Ask,' he says 'and you shall receive.' In fact, you have sought and it has been added to you.

Hilary of Poitiers (c.315–367) writes of the experience of the charisms:

> We begin to have insight into the mysteries of faith, we are able to prophesy and to speak with wisdom. We become steadfast in hope and receive the gifts of healing... These gifts enter us as a gentle rain. Little by little they bear abundant fruit.

Spirit Have to Do with Christian Initiation? (Collegeville: The Liturgical Press, 1991).

Cyril of Jerusalem (c.315–387) also speaks of the charisms in his baptismal lectures: 'Great, omnipotent and admirable is the Holy Spirit in the charisms.' He notes that 'all the laity' have charisms.

Following St Paul's exhortation to especially seek to prophesy, Cyril declares: 'Let each one prepare oneself to receive the heavenly gift (of prophecy),' and, 'God grant that you may be worthy of the charism of prophecy.'

John Chrysostom (c.347–407), commenting on the Syrian liturgy in Antioch notes that the charisms were manifested in connection with the baptismal liturgy and mentions specifically, wisdom, healing, speaking in tongues, prophesy, and other 'wonderful works'. He notes even that 'every church had many who prophesied.' Montague and McDonnell sum up their research with a striking summary.

Thus, from Carthage in North Africa, Poitiers in Gaul, Jerusalem in Palestine, from Caesarea in Cappadocia, from Constantinople, and from Antioch, Apamea, Mabbug, and Cyrrhus in Syria, we have witnesses to the reception of the charisms within the rite of initiation. These are representatives of Latin, Greek, and Syria liturgical traditions. From Antioch, Apamea, Mabbug, and Cyrrhus in Syria we have testimony to a later experiential appropriation of the graces of baptism conferred in infancy.[2]

---

2. *Fanning the Flame,* pp. 20-21.

Chrysostom though, writing in the 5th century, makes the sobering observation that 'the charisms are long gone... The present church is like a woman who has fallen from her former prosperous days. In many respects she retains only the tokens of that ancient prosperity.'[3]

Why, by the fifth century, in at least major portions of the Church, did the Church only retain 'tokens' of her previous charismatic prosperity? Was it because persecution had ceased and it was expected that everyone be a Christian? Were the standards for admitting new Christians lowered? Was the preparation no longer carefully carried out? Did the Montanist heretics give the charisms a bad name?

The Montanist heresy illustrates the wisdom of the Scripture and Church's teaching about the importance of charisms being subject to the discernment of pastoral authority, not to extinguish the Spirit but to test it, holding on to what is sound (1 Thessalonians 5:19-21).

> It is in this sense that the discernment of charisms is always necessary. No charism is exempt from being referred and submitted to the Church's shepherds...so that all the diverse and complementary charisms work together 'for the common good.' (CCC 801)

---

3. All citations are taken from and the original references contained in pp. 16-18 of *Fanning the Flame*.

Whatever the reasons that led to the decline as the life of the Church went on the charisms became mainly associated with the lives of especially holy people, saints, and the charisms are regularly seen in the lives of saints throughout the centuries.

As St Pope John Paul II, and now Pope Emeritus Benedict XVI, continues to lead the proper interpretation and implementation of Vatican II, they both have stressed the importance of rediscovering the universal call to holiness and the universal call to evangelisation. The 'rediscovery' of the charismatic dimension of the Church unfolds in this context.

St John Paul II especially never tired of saying that holiness is for everyone, and that evangelisation is for everyone. It isn't just for special people – saints or missionaries – but that all of us are called to be saints and missionaries.[4]

This is the rediscovery of a biblical and traditional truth that truly has potential to bring an extraordinary 'new springtime' to a Church that desperately needs one.

St John Paul II makes clear that it is very important that this remarkable 'rediscovery' of the charismatic dimension of the Church's constitution be responded to with attention and gratitude

He continues to cry out from the Father's house:

---

4. 'The universal call to holiness is closely linked to the universal call to mission. Every member of the faithful is called to holiness and to mission.' John Paul II, *Redemptoris Missio*, 1990. VIII, 90.

Today, I would like to cry out to all of you gathered here in St Peter's Square and to all Christians: Open yourselves docilely to the gifts of the Spirit! Accept gratefully and obediently the charisms which the Spirit never ceases to bestow on us![5]

May it be so!

---

5. 'This is the day the Lord has made! Holy Father holds historic meeting with ecclesial movements and new communities', *L'Osservatore Romano*, English Language Edition, 3 June 1998, pp. 1-2.

Fanning into Flames the Gifts and Sacraments

Ros Powell

I was speaking at Waterford in Southern Ireland. It was a weekend for leaders, and people who attended local prayer groups. I prayed with this couple and they'd just received the baptism in the Holy Spirit. They asked me if I would pray especially for their young daughter. I think she was about 15, 16, something like that.

I really felt on my heart to say to them, 'Well instead of praying for, could I pray with? Could you bring her tomorrow?' My faith levels were high, so I said, 'If you bring her tomorrow God will heal her.' They told me that she had been born with a birth defect and over the next couple of weeks she had to go into the hospital for a corrective operation. She had one leg shorter than the other which threw her hip out and she couldn't walk properly. They said, 'Oh, I don't think she'll come because she's away from the Mass; she doesn't believe so much in God like she use to when she was little.'

The next morning she walked into the meeting with her parents. I went over to her and I said, 'Can we pray?' I felt the Holy Spirit was saying to me, 'Just pray for healing for her, don't mention to her about going back to the Mass, or the sacraments.' I was just led by the Holy Spirit; we went into an adjoining room and the parents said to me, 'Do you want us to go out?' And I said 'No, I need you to help me in prayer.'

When I prayed for them the day before for the baptism in the Holy Spirit they had both received the gift of tongues. The girl sat down and I did as I had been told and just spoke about healing. I didn't mention to her about coming back to the Lord. Her parents helped me by praying in tongues over her legs. I measured her legs and one leg was much shorter than the other. As I laid my hands on her I could feel the shorter leg moving and growing, I could feel the leg shooting out from the hip sockets, we prayed in tongues for maybe about ten minutes. I asked her, 'How are you?' She said, 'I am fine.' I said, 'Stand up.' She stood up, and she said, 'Wow that's amazing.'

I asked, 'What percentage do you think you're healed?' And she said, 'About ninety per cent.' So I said, 'Okay, let's pray again.' We prayed again, and again she stood up. I said, 'What percentage are you healed?' And she said, 'A hundred per cent.' The shorter leg had grown to the same size as the other one. She could now walk normally without a limp. All of us were crying because Jesus had healed her, which meant that she wouldn't need to go into the hospital to have an operation. As the day went on I noticed that she stayed on and attended Mass which was beautiful. The Lord then released me to talk to her about the Holy Mass. After Mass I went over to her and asked if I could pray with her for the baptism in the Holy

Spirit. She said, 'Yes please.' So I prayed for the baptism in the Holy Spirit and she came back to God, which of course was the greater healing of the two.

Our Church was birthed at Pentecost when the Holy Spirit came in the form of tongues of fire and rested upon the 120 in the Upper Room including Mary the Mother of Jesus. The first gift that they received was the fire, then the next gift that they received was a gift of praying in tongues. Peter – who previously had denied the Lord three times – was changed from a jellyfish to a rock. God gave Peter great boldness. And on that following day when they went into the market place people actually thought that they were drunk. They were drunk in the power of the Holy Spirit and Peter brought 3000 converts to the Lord. They had been baptised in the Holy Spirit.

I usually say to people when I pray with them for the baptism in the Holy Spirit, 'Let's fan into flames your infant baptism and your Confirmation. Everything's already there but sometimes if we are backslidden we have to "fan it into flames and ignite it again" (2 Timothy 1:6).' I know with me when I first received the baptism of the Holy Spirit I felt like a Hoover cleaner (everything is there but in order for it to work it needs plugging into the electricity supply).

I had been baptised and confirmed but l needed to be plugging into God's electricity supply which happened for me when someone laid their hands on me (Acts 8:17; 19:5-6; 28:8).

And the Lord ignited all the sacraments I had received the way He did at Pentecost – the Lord Jesus when He was Ascending up to heaven said I will leave you the comforter (John 14:16) and we all need that comforter (Holy Spirit); when you love someone you just don't tell them once that you love them. If you're besotted with them you keep on telling them that you love them, YOU KEEP ON FANNING THE FLAME.

I have a prison ministry: I found that God gave me a gift of great boldness when I was baptised in the Holy Spirit and the doors of the prison ministry opened up to me. What I find is that when we go into the prisons the Lord gives me such great boldness when I'm speaking to really hardened criminals. I tell them about how God loves sinners, I tell them that God loves to forgive even the vilest sinners. I tell them about Mary Magdalene who had seven demons cast out of her (Luke 8:2); I mention to them about the thief on the cross and on that day he was going to be with the Lord in paradise (Luke 23:39-43).

When I go into the prisons I take three men with me that have served time in prison. They give their testimony and then we say to the lads or the girls, do you want to surrender to Jesus? I would then take them through a prayer where they surrender to Jesus and ask the Holy Spirit to come into their lives. After that we would pray over them individually – Oh! We see miracles; we just see so many miracles! Out of the inmates we speak too we have an 80 per cent response: 80

per cent of them get baptised in the Holy Spirit and receive the gift of tongues. It's wonderful.

When we went to a Category B prison recently – (Category B would be the long-term serious-crime inmates). The punishment system they have in this particular prison we were visiting is what's known as 'lock-up' (they are placed in solitary confinement). The last time we went there, four lads were in lock-up, they were isolated away from the other lads because of unruly behaviour. They are usually highly guarded. On this particular time, I miraculously got permission to go into lock-up and minister to the four lads that were in there. I was able to see them individually in their separate rooms and all four gave their life to Jesus and all four spoke in tongues. You come away and go wow! Wow! Thank you Jesus for setting them free.

Ros Powell (UK) is a speaker with a healing and prison ministry. She speaks regularly at conferences, seminars, retreats and regularly minsters in prisons. She is a member of the English National Service Committee (NSC) the principal co-ordinating organisation of the Catholic Charismatic Renewal (CCR) in England. And is also Spiritual Director to Precious Life – the largest pro-life group in the North of Ireland.

Now when the apostles at Jerusalem heard that Samaria had received the word of God, they sent to them Peter and John, who came down and prayed for them that they might receive the Holy Spirit; for the Spirit had not yet fallen on any of them, but they had only been baptised in the name of the Lord Jesus.

Acts 8:14-16

And when Paul had laid his hands upon them, the Holy Spirit came on them; and they spoke with tongues and prophesied.

Acts 19:6

It is not in our power not to feel or to forget an offence; but the heart that offers itself to the Holy Spirit turns injury into compassion and purifies the memory in transforming the hurt into intercession.

CCC 2843

THE SACRAMENT OF THE ANOINTING
OF THE SICK

This was to fulfil what was spoken by the prophet Isaiah, 'He took our infirmities and bore our diseases.'

Matthew 8:17

[In my name] they will lay their hands on the sick, and they will recover.

Mark 16:18

For I am the Lord, your healer.

Exodus 15:26

'I can pray too'

Fr Timothy Radcliffe OP

One day, some thirty years ago, I was sitting in my room in Blackfriars, Oxford, when the phone rang. It was a friend of mine ringing from hospital, telling me that her 18-year-old son John, had jumped out of the window of a flat on the seventh floor of an apartment block in London in an attempted suicide. I offered to come to the hospital but she said that there was no need since he would soon be dead. I decided to go anyway, since she and her husband would be in deep distress.

John was a charming, sensitive and intelligent young man, artistic and spiritual. But he had been caught taking drugs at his boarding school and been expelled. This had plunged him into a dark hole. His parents decided to take him on a trip around Africa to ease his pain. His mother had gone to collect the plane tickets but on the way back she found a crowd gathered in the road, and in the middle there was her son, his body broken. In hospital they found that he had damaged most of his internal organs, and was not, it seemed, long for this world.

When I arrived in the hospital, to my surprise he was still just alive. The doctor told me that his core temperature was dropping and that he would die soon. I anointed him and whispered, 'John, I am here. We are praying for you.' Somehow he managed to scribble a tiny note in spidery letters, 'I can pray too.' I still have the note. Then his temperature stopped dropping, and slowly death receded. It seemed like a miracle. His recovery took months. I visited him in hospital. He was stretched out on a silk net, like a crucified man. I had to lie on the floor and look up to talk to him.

Two things struck me. His suffering was, in a way, a symptom of his goodness, his sensitivity. Secondly, I felt that the sacrament somehow blessed his inner strength and goodness. St Thomas Aquinas said that grace perfects nature and does not destroy it. Somehow, it seemed that God's strong grace reached down and vitalised the forces of life within him, releasing its self-healing power. God works at the very core of our being, where his grace and our strength are one. John is now married and has a child.

Fr Timothy Radcliffe OP is a Priest and Dominican Friar. He was the Master of the Dominican Order from 1992 to 2001. He is the author of spiritual and religious books, and the winner of the 2007 Michael Ramsey prize for theological writing for his book *What is the Point of Being a Christian?* He travels extensively throughout the world giving retreats, lectures and speaking at conferences.

'Wait, He's Going to Respond to the Sacrament'

Sr Helena Burns FSP

I am telling this story second-hand, but it's such an extraordinary illustration of **God working through matter** (another name for the sacraments) that it has vividly stuck with me through the years.

A good friend of mine, Hannah Carter, was at the bedside of her dying father who was in hospice in a city far from where she lived. Hannah didn't know any of the priests in the area, so she called a local parish to ask for the Sacrament of the Anointing of the Sick.

A priest came, hurriedly did some kind of ceremony that only took a few minutes and left. Hannah had never been present at an anointing of the sick before, but she felt uneasy, almost as though her father had not received 'the Last Rites'. She called another parish priest. When this priest arrived, he performed a lengthy ritual over her father which included something called 'The Commendation of the Dying' (not the '*Condemnation* of the Dying', ha ha).

The Commendation comprises various biblical and deliverance prayers and litanies that recount 'from-death-to-life' Scripture passages.[1] Since her father was unconscious,

---

1. See http://www.ibreviary.com/m/preghiere.php?tipo=Rito&id=371 (last accessed 16 October 2017).

the priest wasn't able to administer Holy Communion, but he gave absolution and a final blessing.

After the sacrament, Hannah was about to rush back to the side of her father to hold his hand and comfort him as she had been doing, but the hospice nurses held her back. 'Wait,' they instructed, having seen this many times before, **'he's going to respond to the sacrament.'** 'What do you mean?' Hannah asked, confused.

'Your father is going to respond to the sacrament. Either he will take a turn for the better for a while, or he will be released.' Sure enough, her father's puckered brow and permanent look of consternation relaxed into a peaceful countenance. He drew one last enormous breath and exhaled every last bit of it as he died. Hannah was at once saddened, relieved and astonished.

The more I study St Pope John Paul II's *Theology of the Body,* the more I see how concrete our God is, what a materialist He is. (He must love matter because He made so much of it, and it's not going away. Rather, there will be a 'new heavens and a **new earth**,' Revelation 21).

John Paul II says in his Theology of the Body that

the spousal meaning of the body is completed by the redemptive meaning on the different roads of life and in different situations: not only in marriage or... virginity, celibacy, but also... in the many kinds of human suffering, indeed, in man's very birth and death. (TOB 102:8)

JP2 did not take up these last two themes in his masterwork, but others have built on it. A new book is entitled *Theology of the Body Extended: the Spiritual Signs of Birth, Impairment and Dying.*

There can be so much fear surrounding the certain prospect of our own death. But we must trust in the One who loves us and Who accompanies us in the person of his priest, 'another Christ', administering the Sacraments at our major life-events: hatched, matched and dispatched.

It is said that the last words of Pope John Paul II were mumbled weakly in Polish, as he struggled to breathe and swallow: **'Let me go to the house of the Father.'** Six hours later, in a comatose state, the great Karol Wojtyla died.

Sr Helena Burns FSP also known as the Media Nun is a member of the Daughters of St Paul, an international congregation founded to communicate God's Word through the media. She is a speaker, author of *He speaks to you*, and Catholic movie reviewer @ http://hellburns.blogspot.co.uk. Sr Helena has developed a Theology of the Body curriculum which she presents to teens, young adults and adults.

Anointing of the Sick
Editor

Nine months after I had been appointed part-time hospital chaplain I was approached after celebrating Mass by a lady with a beaming smile. 'Hi, remember me?' she said in rather loud voice. I smiled politely hoping she would volunteer some more information… and she did (phew!). She said her mum had been on her deathbed at the hospital where I had been called out, and, 'When you came to the bedside you did that Oil thing, on the head and the hands.'

I said, 'The Sacrament of the Sick.' 'Yes', she replied. So I asked, 'How is your mum now?' She said, 'I'm about to go and have lunch with her!' Her mother had made a complete recovery, left hospital and was doing lunch. The daughter said, 'I think I need to start going back to Mass.'

Priests who minister in hospitals can share similar stories about the power of the Sacrament of the Anointing of the Sick. The anointing of the sick is a sacrament that predominantly brings great healing and consolation to the soul, but can also on occasions manifest itself in physical signs. The roots of this sacrament come from Mark 6:13 and the Letter of James when he writes in 5:14 – 'Is any among you sick? Let him call for the elders of the Church, and let them pray over him, anointing him with oil in the name of the Lord.'

How is Jesus Christ present in the Sacrament of Anointing of the Sick?

The Sacrament of the Anointing of the Sick, like all sacraments, is described by Fr Julian Green as 'a particular way in which Jesus Christ makes himself present for a particular purpose through and for the mission of the Church.' When people had sickness and diseases in the times of Jesus, part of his ministry was to heal them through miracles. Why? To reveal who He is – who God is. He healed to reveal his compassion (Matthew 9:36; 14:14). He healed to reveal He had come to give abundance of life (John 10:10), to give a peace the world could not give (John 14:27) and to manifest the glory of God (John 9:3). Sickness became a part of the human condition after the fall of our original parents when sin entered the world. But with the advent of Jesus this was now being transformed, showing that He is the Lord of all Creation! He begins to reverse what the Fall and original sin did and his healings lead to so much more than just a person's physical healing. So when He heals the man born blind (John 9:5-7) He reveals that He is the light of truth; when He heals deafness people are now able to hear the word of God; when He heals someone who is mute it is so they can proclaim the Gospel (Mark 7:32-35). These are all signs to show that the Kingdom of Heaven is a reality

> Care for the sick must have priority over everything else: They should be served as though they were really Christ.
>
> *St Benedict of Nursia*

even now for those who believe. Christ's Body on earth (the Church) continues to give this divine life, an outpouring of heaven's realities, to bring us into deeper intimacy/union with Christ through the sacraments.[1]

I am inspired by what Christ can do through this sacrament and the way in which He reaches out through the priest: after all He is the healer. On one occasion, I was on my ward rounds and came across a lady who was a lapsed Catholic. She had suffered a stroke down her right side. Although she had not been to church in a while I could tell she was a woman of faith, and she responded to the invitation for the Sacrament of Reconciliation. I then asked if she would like to receive the Sacrament of the Sick. Her right hand was curled in on itself and all the fingers were limp so she was unable to use her hand. At the moment the holy oil was put on her right hand with the sign of the cross her hand opened up and she outstretched her arm. She looked at me with shock as she kept opening and closing her hand, stretching her arm back and forward to make sure it had really taken place. 'What

> The Sacrament of the Anointing of the Sick can be received by any Catholic whose health is in a critical state. One can receive the Anointing of the Sick several times in one's life. Therefore it makes sense for young people to ask for this sacrament also, if, for example, they are about to undergo a serious operation.
>
> *YouCat, 243 [1514-1515, 1528-1529]*

---

1. *Sacraments and the Mystery of Christ* (Family Publications, 2009, Maryvale institute, Birmingham) pp. 16-17.

happened?' she asked, bewildered. 'The Holy Spirit has blessed you,' I replied.

There have been occasions of receiving and administering the sacraments when I have received evident signs of God's love, but I have, as well, felt greater temptations and the devil wanting to rob me of those experiences. Which is why the St Michael Prayer or St Patrick's Breastplate would never be too far away from my daily prayers.

Is this sacrament just for the end of life?

There can be a stigma with this sacrament: people think it can only be administered at the end of someone's life. But since Vatican II the Church believes that anyone should receive this sacrament whenever it is needed, when someone has a serious condition. I received it at least five times during my own life when I suffered from depression. I can still recall my first experience of the Sacrament of the Sick:

> Even though I walk through the valley of the shadow of death, I fear no evil; for you are with me.
>
> *Psalm 23:4*

I felt as if a blanket of heat came over me and being overshadowed with love. Later I understood that was the Holy Spirit. Pope Francis has said that being aged 65 or above is good enough reason to receive this sacrament. Some people may use the excuse not to receive it because they believe they are not worthy: well, with that logic we would never receive any of God's sacraments and graces! None of us is worthy, but God in his infinite, beautiful love makes us worthy and invites us to be open to his grace and power working through this sacrament. This anointing, this sacrament, is available for whenever we are struggling with a physical, mental or spiritual illness.

The Bible expert, Francis Selman, writes about how there was no need for sacraments before Christ ascended because people encountered him personally and met his bodily presence. But since his body is now glorified and He is seated at the right hand of God, He has provided the sacraments as the way we have personal contact with him. They are a means for the divine life to enter us, the way that salvation is given to us now through the actions of his body, the Church.[2]

> I was sick and you visited me.
>
> *Matthew 25:3*

When is it difficult for God to do miracles?

In the Gospels there was only one time Jesus could not do many miracles – when He visited his hometown. By their lack of faith they limited everything He wanted to do (Mark 6:1-6). They were unwilling to believe Jesus and let him heal. Similarly, we must have open hearts and believe that God can heal us in whatever form that may take. I have shared stories of physical healings but it is also important to recognise that a lot

---

2. Selman, Francis, *Sacraments and the Mystery of Christ* (Family Publications, 2009, Maryvale institute, Birmingham) pp. 16, 33, 38.

of the time God is doing greater miracles in the soul through this sacrament. I recall once going to the bedside of a dying lady because her relatives had called for the priest as, despite the medical advice, they thought she was not long for this world. However, this lady was anxious and unable to rest. After visiting her and administering this sacrament, and all the other sacraments that are part of the Last Rites, including prayers for the dying, her family later told me that she was at peace and had a holy death. This happens frequently when people are dying and anxious or fearful. After the Sacrament of the Sick they receive deep consolation and a peaceful acceptance of their condition. They prepare themselves for being called back home to God.

The power and the grace

Fr Andrew Apostoli CFR used to tell a true story about a bishop and a priest being called out to a dying Catholic priest. This Catholic priest had left the priesthood, got married and had been estranged from his faith and now wanted to be reconciled back to the Church on his deathbed. As they were walking towards his room, the priest noticed a man in a side room levitating above his bed, identifying it as some kind of demonic activity; he told the bishop that they should both go back and see this patient immediately as they may need their help. But the bishop declined, saying they needed to do what they came to do, attend to their dying brother priest. When they found him, the dying priest made an important confession, received the final sacraments, and was reconciled back to the Church. He died a short time afterwards. As the bishop and priest left, they walked past the side room where the man had been levitating, now back in his bed with nothing to be seen but they heard a voice say out loud, 'We missed his soul.' The brave bishop was undeterred in his mission to reconcile his brother priest back to God's mercy, to save his soul, despite any evil distractions.

A good friend of mine, Fr John Flynn, recounts a story that happened to him. A teenage boy from the Catholic secondary school had contracted meningitis and was in hospital dying. His dad happened to be one of the governors of that school and he contacted Fr John to give his son a blessing. Fr John said he could do more than that: he could give him the Sacrament of the Sick. So even though the young lad was unconscious Fr John ministered the sacrament and left. The following morning, he was contacted to say the young lad had made a complete recovery. It reminds me of the incident in the Gospel when Jesus has pity on the widow's son who had died and was

> Sometimes a person has to become sick in order to recognise what we all – healthy or sick – need more than anything else: God. We have no life except in him. That is why sick people and sinners can have a special instinct for the essential things. Already in the New Testament it was precisely the sick people who sought the presence of Jesus; they tried 'to touch him, for power came forth from him and healed them all' (Luke 6:19).
>
> *YouCat, 241*

being carried out of the city. Jesus touched the young man and ordered him to rise, which he did (Luke 7:11-17). It gives proof to the reality that Christ is able to raise people from their ailments, even from the dead. But are we ready and willing to let him be that intimate with us, to allow that touch, that reaching out, to heal, restore and redeem our souls?

People talk about how it must have been so exciting to live in the days of Jesus when he walked this earth – but 'news flash!' – we have the opportunity to be closer to Jesus than anybody was during his earthy life. He accompanied them, walked with them, embraced them, but now through baptism He lives in us, makes a home in us, and is closer to us then we can even be to ourselves. For example: do you know how many hairs are on your head? He does! (Luke 12:7). And He realises the times in our lives when we need his healing touch to accept whatever our cross may be. Whether it is suffering, illness, or loss, Jesus wants to heal us and bring us peace.

He came to bear and share our sufferings

'My yoke is easy and my burden light' (Matthew 11:30) – Jesus wants to take our crosses and share the pain. There is not a single thing you will ever go through in this life that He has not been through already. The following story illustrates this:

A guy is walking down the road one day and he falls into a man-hole. Now he is stuck in a dark, deep, dingy hole he cannot get out of and screaming for help. A doctor walks down the road, hears the man's cries and looking into the hole says, 'What's the matter?' The guy explains, 'I'm stuck in this dark dingy hole and I cannot get out.' The doctor looks around for a moment and thinks, What can I do? He throws two aspirin into the hole and says 'Here, take those if you get a headache,' and walks off. Next a pastor walks down the road, hears the man's screams, looks into the hole and enquires, 'What's the matter?' The man explains, 'I'm stuck in this dark dingy hole and I cannot get out.' The pastor looks around and thinks to himself, What can I do? He throws a prayer card in and says, 'This might help,' and walks on. Next the man's best friend walks down the road, hears the screams of the man, looks into the hole and says, 'What's the matter?' The man tells his best friend, 'I am stuck in this dark dingy hole and I cannot get out.' The best friend jumps into the hole next to the man. The man says, 'What are you doing, now we're both stuck in this hole!' The best friend says, 'No, I have been here before and I know the way out.' That's Jesus, that's Our Lord, He has been there before and He knows the way out. There is not a single thing you will ever go through in your life that He has not been through already. He wants to share in your pain and your suffering, He wants to help carry the cross.

> The Sacrament of the Anointing of the Sick... expresses God's merciful presence to the sick, the suffering and the aged.
>
> *Pope Francis*

Through your baptism you share in the same Spirit of Christ, the Holy Spirit, the same Spirit that accompanied Jesus during his earthly life, the same Spirit who He taught with, who He healed with, who He miraculously intervened with and who He rose from the dead with. So, because of your baptism there is not a single thing you will ever go through alone. He wants to help you, and help you He does through his sacraments, to bring greater healing, strength and consolation into our lives, into our souls.

God Heals through Medicine

Sr Briege McKenna OSC

There is a beautiful testimony of a little girl who received the Sacrament of the Sick. She had club feet and couldn't walk, although you would never know because she was in a little carriage pushed by her dad. The day after the anointing of the sick there was no physical healing: it didn't happen. Her father, a lawyer, went to his office and his law partner knocked on his office door. 'You know, Joe,' he said, 'I felt so bad when you told me about your little daughter but then I remembered somebody who is a brilliant reconstruction surgeon. Just last night I found his card. I think it would be worth calling him.' Three years later we went back to give a mission in that parish and the child had two normal feet.

In my travels over 40 years with Fr Kevin I have seen miraculous healings through the Sacrament of the Anointing of the Sick – I mean spectacular! We have seen so many people who had tumours and all kinds of physical sicknesses who were healed miraculously and they come back to me and thank me and I'm looking at them thinking it really wasn't me it was the Sacrament of the Anointing!

Witnessing the Power of Jesus to Heal

Fr Kevin Scallon CM

Michael, who worked at the seminary, asked me if I would call to see his next-door neighbour who had cancer. I said yes and he drove me to her home. She was a young married woman who had just returned from hospital. She had cancer of the throat, and the doctor sent her home to be with her family for the last few days of her life. Her husband was there, and their four children, a little girl with three older brothers. I told them who I was, and asked each of them their names.

They all stared at me with a mixture of hope and apprehension. My own heart was empty and I wondered what I could possibly do for this poor skeletal young mother. I have often had that feeling of emptiness in situations like that. I think the Lord allows me to feel this way so that I might realise who the real healer is. All my life, since ever I heard of the Sacrament of the Sick, I had an unusual sense of faith in its efficacy. It has always been a special feature of my ministry as a priest.

So I sat down with them and began to talk to them about why I was there.

'You know that I am a priest,' I said. 'I am here to make Jesus present to you because in the sacraments we meet Jesus himself.'

I looked at the children and said, 'Jesus can heal your mother. Do you believe this?'

'Yes Father,' they said.

They were ready to believe anything. I told them that we read in the Gospels of how Jesus went about doing good and healing the sick.

'Well,' I said, 'He is still doing that in the sacraments of the Church, especially this Sacrament of the Anointing of the Sick and the Holy Eucharist.'

I explained how I would pray special prayers, lay my hands on their mother, anoint her with the Holy Oil of the Sick, and ask Jesus to heal her. They were all full of hope and sure faith that Jesus would come and care for their poor sick mother. It is always important that the priest gives a short teaching on the reality of the presence of Jesus in the sacrament. Very many people have little understanding of this. When I had finished, I assured them that I would continue to pray for their mother, and for all of them, especially during Holy Mass. I left and the visit faded into memory.

Thirty years later, still at the seminary, a woman called to see me.

As often happens, she said, 'Do you remember me, Father?'

To which I honestly replied, 'I am sorry; I do not.'

'You came to see me thirty years ago when I was dying of cancer, and you prayed with me and anointed me in the Sacrament of the Sick.'

'Oh yes,' I replied, 'now I remember.'

'Well,' she said, 'from the moment you ministered to me, I immediately began to get better, and in a short time I was completely healed and restored to normal health, and I have never been sick since. I often intended to come to see you, but I never seemed to get around to it.' She stood there a picture of health, her husband at home, her children grown with families of their own.

I always encourage priests to minister this wonderful sacrament, no matter how busy they are at that moment. It is the healing ministry of Christ himself, and we must always provide him with the opportunity of easing the sufferings of the poor. I have witnessed the power of Jesus to heal every kind of sickness including depression, addictions, and an abundance of hidden ailments that even the wonderful skills of doctors of modern medicine could not reach. My expectation of this sacrament is that people will be healed, and not the opposite. It is my firm conviction that when we priests bring the healing Christ to people through this sacrament our merciful Saviour always does something for them. But it is the presence of Christ himself, and the peace and fortitude that only He can impart, that makes the greatest difference in the lives of the poor and afflicted.

Fr Kevin J. Scallon CM is a priest of the Vincentian Community, international author and speaker who initially ministered in England and Nigeria. In 1976 he started the Intercession for Priests in Ireland and along with Sr Briege McKenna has travelled extensively around the world ministering to priests and lay people.

Heal the sick, raise the dead, cleanse lepers, cast out demons. You received without payment; give without payment.

Matthew 10:8

The Anointing of the Sick imparts consolation, peace, and strength and unites the sick person, in his precarious situation and his sufferings, with Christ in a profound way. For the Lord experienced our fears and bore our pains in his body. For many people the Anointing of the Sick brings about physical healing. But if God should decide to call someone home to himself, he gives him in the Anointing of the Sick the strength for all the physical and spiritual battles on his final journey. In any case, the Anointing of the Sick has the effect of forgiving sins.

YouCat, 245 [1520-1523, 1532]

I will bless you... so that you will be a blessing.

Genesis 12:2b

Conclusion

Sometimes when I pray with people images and pictures come to mind. The images are almost like a plasma screen in my mind where the picture/scene unfolds. I explain that St Paul talks about this in one of his letters about the gifts of the Holy Spirit (1 Corinthians 12:7-10), which Dr Ralph Martin explains so well in the chapter on the Sacrament of Confirmation.

For example, on one occasion I had been asked to visit a seriously ill patient in the hospital and after he had gone to confession and received the Sacrament of the Anointing of the Sick, we prayed together. During this time of prayer, I received a couple of images: I said that if they meant anything to him he could meditate upon them, but if not, just let them go. At this point we had both been joined by his daughter. I described the first image: in it I saw him at the top of a snowy mountain, dressed as a mountaineer and I felt God was saying to him that He takes us to where we need to be. In the second image, he had an empty butterfly net and was trying to make a catch. I felt a strong sense he was meant to be open to discovering the beauty and wonder God had for him. This image, I believed, also represented new life for him (as that is what a butterfly does – brings new life from a caterpillar and cocoon state). After I shared these images he seemed deep in thought but his daughter was excited. She explained that her dad was a mountain climber (he had climbed three mountains) and that when she was a child they used to go butterfly-catching. The images resonated with them both and seemed to be a source of strength for the situation he was in.

God knows us so well, in the intimate details of our lives. He speaks his language of love into our hearts in a way we can best understand. There is not a single thing in our lives He does not want to be part of, reclaim and transform through his love. Everything matters to him because He seeks our holiness (Leviticus 20:26). Please never make the mistake I made by thinking you need to be good enough before you can go to him. He meets us in our brokenness and our vulnerability because He loves us so much. Holiness, as we have seen in this book, is surrendering our entire life to God, especially our weaknesses, and allowing him to transform us in His love. The more we give him, the more He transforms and the holier we become, just as St Paul explained, 'It is no longer I who live but Christ in me' (Galatians 2:20).

Our first vocation is to be holy, to show forth God's image to the world, by being transformed into the image of God's only Son, Jesus (CCC 1877). And this happens in a profound way through the sacraments. As we have read, the infusion, the outpouring of his divine life and love through the sacraments is meant to fill our souls and impact our lives in such a way that we can be the face of Christ to our neighbour, bringing his love and healing to our families, neighbourhoods, nations, and out into the world. And don't forget, the deeper your union with Christ the more you share in the divine intimacy that the Son shares with the Father and Holy Spirit (CCC 850). But it is down to us – how open and receptive our hearts are to the sacraments – whether they will produce great fruit in our lives. Our faith, trust and openness is key! (CCC 1098, 2563).

I hope through reading this book you have been inspired by the testimonies of the contributors. And that if you did not already know, you do now, that God has amazing plans for you – through the sacraments that make us holy. He wants your soul to shimmer, to shine and to radiate his beauty out into the world.

Some of the stories in this book may have resonated with you. Or maybe it has not happened for you, but the testimonies in this book are inspiring you to embark on that journey... or maybe you feel you're not in a position to begin. But here's the thing, you're only one confession away from receiving an outpouring of this Divine love and life to set you on your way. Depending on your current lifestyle it may involve a radically brave decision to change your way of living for the sake of the Gospel and all that God wants to do in your life. After all, God wants you to be a **saint**!

But there are never any easy routes to such a high calling. To follow Christ is the way of the cross (Mark 8:34), but through that cross is eternal life. As St Rose of Lima put it, 'Apart from the cross there is no other ladder by which we may get to heaven.' But as we have seen in this book, despite the sacrifices and difficulties we undertake for God, He provides us with the deeply rooted love, joy, peace and strength to endure. That, no person, place or thing can take away from us.

May I make a suggestion? If you haven't yet experienced all that God wants you to have in the sacraments, let Our Lady help you. She was a great source of strength for me when I felt I was just not good enough to approach God. She bought me to him. Over the years I have received so much grace from God through her intercession. As your spiritual mother (John 19:27) she wants to assist and lead you to encounters with her Son. When the angel Gabriel appeared to her he announced she was full of grace (Luke 1:28): not half-full, a little bit of grace, but full of grace. She knew what it was to overflow with the love of God, to be holy. As the Immaculate Conception, through the Incarnation, at Pentecost, she accompanied the disciples and apostles by helping to prepare them to receive the Holy Spirit. She would have helped them understand and comprehend the Holy Spirit's fullness, as one who already knew the intimacy and love of the Father. If she was there for them, she will be there for you, if you invite her.

A big heartfelt thanks to all the contributors of this book: all those who have written, shared or contributed testimonies to help bring you into a deeper personal relationship with God through his life-giving sacraments, lived out in love and service to him and your neighbour.

And never forget, you're only ever a few decisions away from being the person God wants you to be – so you're only ever a few decisions away from being a saint!

As St Catherine of Siena says:

If you are what you are meant to be, you will set the whole world on fire!

Chapter Collaborators

Barbara Reed Mason (USA) is an evangelist, catechist, artist and author who has been involved in faith formation for over 25 years. In the UK and internationally, Barbara gives retreats, talks, Bible studies and courses in the faith. She is the author of the *Kerygma Bible Retreat* and the study guide *Is Religion Necessary? And Other Questions.* She has played a significant role in this book being produced.

Fr Julian Green (UK) is a priest of the Archdiocese of Birmingham currently serving in three parishes in Stoke-on-Trent. He was a former Catholic Chaplain to the University of Birmingham and Seminary Lecturer at Oscott College (Birmingham) specialising in Ecclesiology and Mariology. He is a member of the Society of St John Vianney.

Charlotte Hibbert (UK) is a Lay Chaplain at St Bede's College Manchester, and Young Adults Coordinator for the Reignite project in Salford Diocese. Charlotte is an experienced speaker and workshop leader and with her husband Christopher delivers marriage preparation courses within the diocese. Recently they have both been involved in the promotion of 'Family is Sacred' by the Catholic Bishops of England and Wales. Charlotte and Christopher have three children.

Mary's Meals

www.marysmeals.org.uk